RESPOND

Christ-centered. Discipleship.

Discover Meaning.

Christ-centered Discipleship. Part II

RESPOND: CHRIST-CENTERED. DISCIPLESHIP.
By Chris Browne

First printing July 25, 2014

ISBN-13: 978- 0615992396 (WheatonPress.com)
ISBN-10: 0615992390

This title available at Amazon.com or wherever fine books are sold. Please visit the publisher online at www.WheatonPress.com for more books in this series, classroom or small group discounts, and other resources designed to equip you in your discipleship journey.

For my wife, who for the past two decades has walked with me as together we have continued to learn what it means to respond to Jesus.

CONTENTS

INTRODUCTION

We Are Invited to Respond

In modern times there are countless tools, books, and resources that are designed to help Christians grow in almost every area of life imaginable. In some ways it is easy to be overwhelmed by the number of discipleship materials, programs and initiatives that are available to us. With the number of publishing companies, missions agencies, podcasts, radio stations, schools, and churches that are producing all of this material, it is startling to learn from recent studies that the majority of those who claim to be Christians could not identify what the end result of following Jesus is supposed to produce.[1]

If we were to apply every spiritual growth program that we currently have available, what should our end result look like? How should it change or transform our families, communities or churches? What is discipleship supposed to produce?

According the Barna study, when asked similar questions, nearly 50% of Christians in America would not venture a guess. According to that same study, nearly nine out of ten churches did not even have a written definition of spiritual maturity. Without a clear definition of where we are going, how will we know if we get there?

DIRECTIONALLY CHALLENGED

I enjoy traveling, and I find myself in new cities on a regular basis. I am also directionally challenged. I know what it feels like to get into a rental car with a loose set of directions jotted on a piece of paper or a napkin with no real idea what my destination looks like or how to get there. As a result, I also know how it feels to make a wrong turn (or two) and to feel gripped by the realization that I am lost (again). I know what it feels like to be at a busy intersection praying for wisdom as the panic quickens my pulse, and the feeling of helplessness erodes my confidence. I know the feeling of speeding up or slowing down or talking to myself out loud while I'm alone in the car hoping that somehow my surroundings will make sense and I will feel at peace again.

A few years ago, my wife bought me my first GPS device. It was a life-changing moment. No longer am I destined to choose between wandering in circles on my own or asking random strangers for directions. Now with the touch of a few buttons, I can enter a destination and my GPS will calculate a route. When I take wrong turns, the GPS recalculates a route back to my intended destination. But the GPS can not function to full capacity until I communicate my final destination by clearly typing it into the mechanism.

8. Christ-centered.

Many of us have been driving a spiritual route without a clear idea of where we are supposed to end up or if we are even on the right road. We know the frustration that accompanies the questions: Where are we going? What is the final destination?

REFLECTIONS OF THE MASTER

Growing up, my definition of discipleship was too narrow. Somewhere in the mix of attending church and Bible college, I learned that the definition of a disciple is to be a follower. But in reality, a disciple is defined as a reflection of the original. The New Testament word for disciple is the word *mathetes*. It means, "a learner or student of a master." The Greek word *mimētēs* means, "to emulate or to imitate." In context it means to become an imitator or a reflection of something or someone and it is used seven times in the New Testament to describe the result of discipleship.

When you connect the concepts of a disciple being "a learner or student of a master" with the goal of learning to becoming an imitation or exact copy of their teacher it gives a clearer context to Christ's words in Matthew 10:24-25 when He states that a student will become like his teacher. In a direct reference to the rabbinical system of discipleship of His time, Jesus reminds His new disciples that they are called to become His reflections; to become just like Him.

Inherent in Christ's definition of being a disciple is the reality that simply following Jesus is not intended to be the end unto itself. We are called to become his reflections.

That is why the rest of the New Testament writers use the word *mimētēs* to connect the concept of imitating God with the goal of spiritual maturity.

> Therefore be imitators of God, as dearly loved children.
>
> Ephesians 5:1 (ESV)

Not only is *mimētēs* used by Paul in Ephesians 5 to clarify the definition of spiritual maturity, he also uses it as his definition of discipleship in his invitation to the churches in Corinth and Thessalonica inviting them to imitate him as he imitates Christ:

> Therefore I urge you to imitate me.
>
> 1 Corinthians 4:16 (NIV)

> Be imitators of me, as I am of Christ.
>
> 1 Corinthians 11:1 (ESV)

> And you became imitators of us and of the Lord....
>
> 1 Thessalonians 1:6a (ESV)

10. Christ-centered.

DIRECTIONALLY FOCUSED

"Yoke" is a term that is often lost in translation outside of an understanding of how a Jewish rabbi would have used this word during the time of Christ. Today we typically hear sermons about how "yoke" refers to a large wooden contraption placed over the necks of oxen, but that is only part of the image that will give us an accurate understanding of how Christ meant it.

In the time of Christ, the word "yoke" referred to the body of teaching that a rabbi expected his followers to be able to apply to their lives and to reproduce in the lives of others. Most rabbis prided themselves in how difficult or complicated their yoke was to the minds of the average observer or individual who desired to follow their interpretation of the law. From this perspective, the image of a large, cumbersome wooden yoke that lays heavy on the back and neck of an ox is an accurate image. This was the typical rabbinical yoke placed on the backs of the people. In fact, from the perspective of the average rabbi, the more complex their yoke, and the more difficult it was to follow their interpretation of the law in order to attempt to please God and win His favor, then the more prestigious it was to be one of their disciples. The truth was, as Christ noted on many different occasions, the conventional teachers of the law began to find more pride in their religious efforts than in their true desire to please God.

Like just about everything else about Jesus, His yoke was different. He promised that His yoke would be easy to understand and apply. Early on in his ministry with his disciples, Jesus promised to those who were listening to Him that His rabbinical yoke would be easy to understand and apply. [2]

In other words, Jesus promised to lay out his process for discipleship in a way that was easy to understand and apply to our lives.

This resource is designed to present Christ's invitations and His process in an understandable format and to give you an opportunity to hear, understand, and apply the Word of God to your life in a way that is organized and understandable. The goal is that together through these pages, we will follow Christ and uncover His simple, reproducible, and sustainable process for becoming his imitator and for equipping others to do the same.

Through this process we will see that spiritual growth is not about trying harder to follow the rules; it is not about making lists or working hard to modify our behavior. Spiritual maturity is about becoming reflections of the fullness of Christ; spiritual maturity is learning to hear His voice and respond to it.

12. Christ-centered.

CHAPTER 1

INVITED TO RESPOND

Before we attempt to uncover Christ's process for making disciples, we need to examine and understand why His invitation to become a disciple is actually a pretty big deal in and of itself.

If you are like me, there are a few passages throughout Scripture, as well as several actions or responses of Christ recorded in the Gospels, that seem odd, or at least puzzling.

For me, one of those events was the moment when Christ was walking along the shore of the Sea of Galilee and issued His invitation to the fishermen to become his disciples. Matthew records what occurred that day:

As Jesus was walking beside the Sea of Galilee, he saw two brothers, Simon called Peter and his brother Andrew. They were casting a net into the lake, for they were fishermen. "Come, follow me," Jesus said, "and I will send you out to fish for people." At once they left their nets and followed him.

Going on from there, he saw two other brothers, James son of Zebedee and his brother John. They were in a boat with their father Zebedee, preparing their nets. Jesus called them, and immediately they left the boat and their father and followed him.

Matthew 4:18-22 (NIV)

After reading this passage, I have often wondered, "Did Jesus glow in the dark?" Perhaps those paintings of Jesus with a radiant heart were more accurate than I'd care to admit. Because what other reason could there be for four fishermen in the middle of a workday with their dad to drop everything and follow some guy walking along the beach just because He invited them to follow Him? For years, I figured that either these guys were slackers looking to get out of work or that Jesus must have magically glowed in the dark.

However, as cool as it might be to imagine, the image of glowing Jesus is disqualified by the description we receive of him through the prophet Isaiah, who wrote:

He had no beauty or majesty to attract us to him, nothing in his appearance that we should desire him.

Isaiah 53:2b (NIV)

14. Christ-centered.

What would have caused these fishermen and the others who followed him to literally leave everything behind? And why don't the Gospels have any record that those around them were not upset about it? To understand the answer to that question, we need to delve into Jewish history and the promises God made to the nation of Israel all the way back near the beginning of the Old Testament.

CHOSEN BY GOD

In Deuteronomy, Moses records the history of Israel for the people to remember as they complete their journey into the Promised Land. After being rescued by God from slavery in Egypt they have wandered in the desert for forty years and watched the generation of people who had previously been led to the edge of the land promised to them by God die after failing to trust Him and sinning through their lack of faith.

In Deuteronomy, God speaks through Moses to remind a new generation of His promises and in the seventh chapter we read that God chose the nation of Israel to be set aside for His purposes:

> For you are a people holy to the Lord your God. The Lord your God has chosen you out of all the peoples on the face of the earth to be his people, his treasured possession.
>
> Deuteronomy 7:6 (NIV)

At first glance, God's choice could seem confusing or even offensive. Why would God select an entire nation of people to become his "treasured possession?" What made them so special as to attract that type of favor and attention? Moses answers that question and elaborates:

> The Lord did not set his affection on you and choose you because you were more numerous than other peoples, for you were the fewest of all peoples. But it was because the Lord loved you and kept the oath he swore to your ancestors that he brought you out with a mighty hand and redeemed you from the land of slavery, from the power of Pharaoh king of Egypt. Know therefore that the Lord your God is God; he is the faithful God, keeping his covenant of love to a thousand generations of those who love him and keep his commandments.
>
> Deuteronomy 7:7-9 (NIV)

The nation of Israel was chosen not because of anything they had done to deserve God's favor, but because of God's love and His desire to show His glory through them, and through His faithfulness throughout their journey of redemption.

Their story is an illustration of our own story. God, who is rich in mercy, grace, and love, redeems us when we have done nothing to deserve His attention[1] and is faithful to us when our hearts rebel against His.[2]

16. Christ-centered.

God's instructions to the people of Israel through Moses did not stop at verse nine with His unconditional covenant to love and to be faithful to the nation He chose. His promise that they will be his people and He will be their God was unconditional. His promise that they would experience the benefits of obedience to Him and His words was conditional upon their obedience:

> Therefore, take care to follow the commands, decrees and laws I give you today.
>
> If you pay attention to these laws and are careful to follow them, then the Lord your God will keep his covenant of love with you, as he swore to your ancestors. He will love you and bless you and increase your numbers. He will bless the fruit of your womb, the crops of your land—your grain, new wine and olive oil—the calves of your herds and the lambs of your flocks in the land he swore to your ancestors to give you.
>
> You will be blessed more than any other people; none of your men or women will be childless, nor will any of your livestock be without young.
>
> The Lord will keep you free from every disease. He will not inflict on you the horrible diseases you knew in Egypt, but he will inflict them on all who hate you.
>
> Deuteronomy 7:11-15 (NIV)

Those are some amazing promises God gave to Israel if they followed His laws carefully. They were promised large families and abundant crops. Everything in their life would experience the blessing of God more than any other people on earth. Why? Was it because they were special? Or because somehow they deserved this privilege and honor? No, because God desired that they would be a living illustration to the world of what it is to reflect and honor Him and His will. He chose them, not to bring glory to them, but that through their obedience they would bring glory to Him.

Check out this amazing explanation and promise from God in the first few verses of Deuteronomy 8:

> Be careful to follow every command I am giving you today, so that you may live and increase and may enter and possess the land the Lord promised on oath to your ancestors. Remember how the Lord your God led you all the way in the wilderness these forty years, to humble and test you in order to know what was in your heart, whether or not you would keep his commands. He humbled you, causing you to hunger and then feeding you with manna, which neither you nor your ancestors had known, to teach you that man does not live on bread alone but on every word that comes from the mouth of the Lord. Your clothes did not wear out and your feet did not swell during these forty years. Know then in your heart that as a man disciplines his son, so the Lord your God disciplines you.
>
> Deuteronomy 8:1-5 (NIV)

If you read the first book in this series on Christ-centered discipleship, then you may remember pride is a reflection of the enemy of God, and we are called to reflect the humility demonstrated by Christ. Here, God is helping the nation of Israel make sense of their past forty years. He was not looking for a transactional obedience of blessing in payment for their actions. Rather, He desired that their hearts would belong to Him. So much was His desire that they learn to trust Him that He gave them a forty-year illustration of His power by feeding them and by not allowing the normal physical consequences of wandering in the wilderness for four decades. The next time they faced a large obstacle, that of entering into the Promised Land, they would be able to look back and say, "The God who promised to feed us for the past forty years is big enough to conquer the enemies in the land He promised us." Through their trials, they would learn to trust; through their trust, they would learn to love; and that love would be their motivation for obedience. He did not want to redeem their actions alone; He desired their hearts.

The point of the law was not for the nation of Israel to earn rewards but to learn humility. It was not for their hearts to grow proud at their accomplishments, but to grow humble at their dependency. Watch as God through Moses warns them of their propensity to enjoy His blessings while forgetting Him:

> Be careful that you do not forget the Lord your God, failing to observe his commands, his laws and his decrees that I am giving you this day.
>
> Otherwise, when you eat and are satisfied, when you build fine houses and settle down, and when your

herds and flocks grow large and your silver and gold
increase and all you have is multiplied, then your
heart will become proud and you will forget the Lord
your God, who brought you out of Egypt, out of the
land of slavery.

Deuteronomy 8:11-14 (NIV)

Watch the repeated emphasis to remember that it was
God who is responsible and who is at the center of His
blessings and not them.

He led you through the vast and dreadful wilderness,
that thirsty and waterless land, with its venomous
snakes and scorpions. He brought you water out of
hard rock.

He gave you manna to eat in the wilderness,
something your ancestors had never known, to
humble and test you so that in the end it might go
well with you.

Deuteronomy 8:15-16 (NIV)

The reminder of the chapter is bookended with another
admonition that would prove to be prophetic.

You may say to yourself, "My power and the
strength of my hands have produced this wealth for
me." But remember the Lord your God, for it is he
who gives you the ability to produce wealth, and so
confirms his covenant, which he swore to your
ancestors, as it is today.

Deuteronomy 8:17-18 (NIV)

Later, the prophet Jeremiah would record that this warning was prophetic in that the nation of Israel did not walk in obedience and they did not listen or pay attention to the words of Moses.

> I gave them this command: Obey me, and I will be your God and you will be my people. Walk in obedience to all I command you that it may go well with you. But they did not listen or pay attention; instead, they followed the stubborn inclinations of their evil hearts. They went backward and not forward. From the time your ancestors left Egypt until now, day after day, again and again I sent you my servants the prophets. But they did not listen to me or pay attention. They were stiff-necked and did more evil than their ancestors.
>
> Jeremiah 7:23-26 (NIV)

Before we judge Israel for their disobedience, we should ponder how often we are guilty of the same thing. How often do we experience the blessings and grace of God and then forget Him and claim His glory for our own? How often could Jeremiah's words about the hearts of the Israelites be written about our own hearts?

Unfortunately for the nation of Israel, there were consequences for their disobedience. Just as there was a promise of what would occur if the people obeyed God, there was also a promise of what would take place if they disobeyed Him:

> If you ever forget the Lord your God and follow
> other gods and worship and bow down to them, I
> testify against you today that you will surely be
> destroyed.
>
> Deuteronomy 8:19 (NIV)

But instead of immediately elaborating on the
consequences of what would happen, Moses reminds
them of the centrality of the law and their obedience to it,
and he reminds the people of God's blessing and
provides key information that will help us understand
what caused the fishermen to drop their nets and follow
Christ.

> So if you faithfully obey the commands I am giving
> you today—to love the Lord your God and to serve
> him with all your heart and with all your soul—then I
> will send rain on your land in its season, both
> autumn and spring rains, so that you may gather in
> your grain, new wine and olive oil. I will provide
> grass in the fields for your cattle, and you will eat and
> be satisfied.
>
> Deuteronomy 11:13-15 (NIV)

That seems straightforward. The people of God must
faithfully obey God's commands and love Him with all of
their heart and soul to receive the benefit. But again, God
reminds them that it is not about their actions; it is about
their hearts. Watch what God promises will result if their
hearts turn away from Him.

> Be careful, or you will be enticed to turn away and
> worship other gods and bow down to them. Then

the Lord's anger will burn against you, and he will shut up the heavens so that it will not rain and the ground will yield no produce, and you will soon perish from the good land the Lord is giving you.

Deuteronomy 11:16-17 (NIV)

Based on the words recorded in Deuteronomy, my preference is to be on the receiving end of God's favor and not His anger. Yet, Israel, disobeyed. Their hearts turned away from God, and their actions followed with disobedience. The result was that God kept His promise and they were removed from the land.

PROMISE OF GOD

They were enslaved. They were persecuted. They were abused. They were brutalized through the Babylonian and the Assyrian conquests and resulting exiles. By the time we rejoin our fishermen, they were only a few generations removed from that time when Israel finally returned to their land. During the time of Jesus, Israel was still experiencing life under the occupation of the Romans. Every day, they felt the stinging pain of life apart from the blessing of God. Every day they heard ringing in their ears the words of Moses recorded in the rest of Deuteronomy 11 as a warning and a hopeful reminder:

Fix these words of mine in your hearts and minds; tie them as symbols on your hands and bind them on your foreheads. Teach them to your children, talking about them when you sit at home and when you walk along the road, when you lie down and when you get up. Write them on the doorframes of your houses and on your gates, so that your days and the days of your children may be many in the land the Lord swore to give your ancestors, as many as the days that the heavens are above the earth.

Deuteronomy 11:18-21 (NIV)

The fishermen were in the Promised Land, but they experienced the blessing of God only in part. They were under Roman occupation, but they were children of the generation who believed that by fulfilling the obligation recorded in verses 18-21, they would experience the blessings of God not in part, but in full.

That commitment produced a system of education led by those who had dedicated their lives to studying, understanding, and conveying the words of God. In their steadfastness to careful discipline and obedience, they clung to the assurance that God would remain faithful. One day a leader would arise from among them whose devotion to God the Father would enable freedom from slavery and the full blessings of right relationship with God.

We see this promise of God's faithfulness in Jeremiah 30:

This is what the Lord says:
"I will restore the fortunes of Jacob's tents
and have compassion on his dwellings;
the city will be rebuilt on her ruins,
and the palace will stand in its proper place.

24. Christ-centered.

From them will come songs of thanksgiving
and the sound of rejoicing.

I will add to their numbers,
and they will not be decreased;
I will bring them honor,
and they will not be disdained.

Their children will be as in days of old,
and their community will be established before me;
I will punish all who oppress them.
Their leader will be one of their own;
their ruler will arise from among them.

I will bring him near and he will come close to me—
for who is he who will devote himself
to be close to me?' declares the Lord.

So you will be my people, and I will be your God."
Jeremiah 30:22 (NIV)

THE AGE OF THE RABBI

It is with this promise in mind that we pick up the
story of Jesus' encounter with the fishermen. Every man
and woman growing up in the Galilee region of Israel
knew the promise of Moses and the promise of Jeremiah.

These young fishermen on the northern shores of
the Galilee were only a few generations removed from the
pain the ensued when God's people failed to follow and
keep His commandments. They heard stories around the
dinner table and warnings in the streets as well as the
synagogues of what would take place if they did not

carefully understand and apply the words of God to their life.

Every day they experienced the results of former generations who had forgotten to live according to the law of God and rebelled against Him. The existence of the Romans was a constant reminder of what happens when God's people rebel against Him. They longed to change their circumstances. They paid taxes to a Roman Caesar who claimed to be a god. Every time a Roman soldier showed cruelty to them or a member of their family, they were reminded of the dangers and results of not following the law of Moses to the letter.

They longed to experience the benefits of obedience and be known as the people of God again. And one of the ways that they hoped the change would occur was through the rabbinical system.

NEVER FORGET

Change would only take place when a generation arose who had been trained in the words of God and who would in turn train others. This meant that in every Jewish community there were two things that were sacred and honored. The first was to have a copy of the written word of God in order to study it and apply it to every area of their lives.

The second was the possibility of being chosen worthy to be trained by a rabbi and even achieve the honor of becoming a rabbi. Rabbis were the ones entrusted to bring the people back to the words of God. It is important to understand that rabbis were not priests. The role of a priest was different than that of a rabbi.

Priests were the mediators between God and man. Priests could only be from the tribe of Levi and it was their responsibility to offer the sacrifices, and to serve in the temple. But there was an entire system of religious leaders, scribes, and Pharisees who played important roles in the Jewish religious system at the time of Christ who were not priests and who were not from the tribe of Levi.

One of the key religious leaders was the Jewish rabbi. Rabbis could be from any tribe and were not limited to the tribe of Levi. To become a rabbi was considered the highest honor that a young man not born into the tribe of Levi could aspire to. If you were a Jewish mom or Jewish dad, it was your dream that your son might be considered worthy to become a rabbi.

In the New Testament, Paul, in his second letter to Timothy, exhorted the young man to study that he might be approved unto God, a workman who did not need to be ashamed but who could correctly divide the words of God's truth.[1]

The rabbinical writings inform us that to become a rabbi would have been the goal of every good, young Jewish boy from the moment that he could begin to understand the significance of what it meant. For every parent the dream was that their son might one day study the word of God as the disciple of a rabbi and that he might one day honor their family by becoming a rabbi. This was an age of discipleship, and it was an honor in Jewish culture to be considered qualified to be a disciple, who would in turn one day be entrusted to be a rabbi.

WHY?

Why was it considered such an honor? Because if the Jewish nation was to again receive the blessing of God and be freed from under the rule of Roman occupation, it would be through the nation returning to an understanding and obedience to the law of God. And that meant studying God's word night and day in order to understand, obey, and teach it to perfection.

This meant careful study, division, and ordering of the text under a rabbi who had devoted his entire life to understanding and teaching the words of God. To the priests was entrusted the sacrificial system that paid for the sins of their past, to the rabbis was entrusted the future of the nation through clear teaching and application of the law.

28. Christ-centered.

We see this lived out time and again throughout the Gospels when we read that the Jewish religious leaders and the teachers of the law were standing around arguing about the law and which law was the most important. These were men who had devoted their entire lives to attempting to figure out what laws were the most important ones to follow and obey in order for God to bring them back into His good graces and for them to begin receiving His blessings again, and it was the dream of every good Jewish family that their son would have what it took to become a rabbi.

A GENERATION OF DISCIPLES

At the age of five, every Jewish child would go to school to begin memorizing the law of God under the tutelage of a local rabbi. The goal was to ensure that the next generation understood how to approach God through His law and that they would not repeat the sins of the previous generation.

By the ages of 7-9, those children considered to be at the top of their class and who showed the promise that one day they could become a rabbi would advance to the next level of school and memorization. Those who failed to show promise were sent back home to work in the family business. They would still attend synagogue during the nights and weekends, but by that age many had already demonstrated that they did not have what it took to become a rabbi.

Those who advanced began the next level by memorizing the entire law as well as the prophets using learning tools that ensured that they did not just memorize the words, but every aspect and concept as well. For example rabbis would play games with their students by asking them questions to measure their grasp of the text. Between the ages of 7-9 common questions from a rabbi might include, "Name each of the birds listed in the first five books of the Torah - in order."

Those students who excelled and showed promise through the ages of 7-9 were asked to continue; those who failed were sent back home to the family business and considered not worthy of the rabbi's investment of time.

Between the ages of 10-12 the real memorization would begin as the young child would begin mastering the entire Old Testament by memory. In addition, the Socratic method of teaching would be introduced as their cognitive skills increased and they could begin to demonstrate higher levels of abstract thinking.

One method of learning was based on a rabbi asking a student a question with a vague reference to a specific passage or verse in the Old Testament and waiting for the child's response. The child, in order to demonstrate understanding of the question and mastery of the concept would then ask a question in return. Back and forth this process would go as the rabbis again weeded potential disciples from those who would be sent

30. Christ-centered.

back to the family business.

What is particularly interesting about this process is that while we know very little about the childhood of Christ, the one thing that we do learn is that at the age of twelve His parents discover Him in the temple doing what... asking questions. And the religious leaders of His day are amazed at His questions. Without the understanding of the Jewish educational system that passage does not make a lot of sense, but with the understanding that Jesus was a normal Jewish boy who was advancing through school it makes a lot of sense.

Between the ages of 13-15, if a young man had not been sent home yet, they could begin the process of considering which rabbi to ask if they could follow. They would have one chance. If the rabbi said yes, then the youngster would have the honor of becoming a disciple who would devote the next fifteen years of their life learning to become an imitator of their rabbi. Then after fifteen years of being a disciple and over twenty five years of constant study, around the age of thirty, if their rabbi considered them worthy they would have the opportunity to be known as a rabbi and to begin making their own disciples.

To say that it was simply an honor to become a disciple would be a gross understatement, because it was through discipleship alone that the nation could be transformed. It was through the careful study of the law and the teaching of the rabbis that the nation of Israel had the opportunity to receive the promised blessings of God again, and it was the desire of every young Jewish boy that they would be considered worthy to become a rabbi.

That is why when a rabbi came walking alongside their boats one morning and issued an invitation to follow Him, the young fishermen understood the significance of what He was inviting them to and they dropped their nets and joined Him.

The invitation of a rabbi was a signal that the rabbi believed they had what it took to become a protector of Israel. Jesus' summons as a rabbi to the fisherman was a signal of His confidence in them to become His disciples, to learn from Him and then be entrusted to teach others for the purpose of leading the people back to the blessing of God. The invitation of a rabbi was the hope for the nation.

It invited a response.

In light of the context of the time, how could the young fishermen have responded to the invitation of a rabbi any differently?

A GENERATION WITHOUT DISCIPLES

For the most part, statistics and studies tell us that unlike the young fishermen for whom the concept of discipleship was not only the norm, but one that was regarded with prestige, we live in an age without disciples

32. Christ-centered.

and without an understanding of why discipleship matters or what discipleship is supposed to produce.

The church marketing machine tells us that churches in North America are growing larger numerically. However, while there are increasing numbers in attendance, there are decreasing numbers of disciples. George Barna tells us that less than one in four Christians meet the biblical standard for being a disciple, and the Gallup Organization tells us that less than one out of every five people who regularly attend church have been asked about their spiritual growth in the past six months.

It seems the Apostle Paul's words to the Corinthian church fit us all too well:

> Even if you had ten thousand guardians in Christ, you do not have many spiritual fathers, for in Christ Jesus I became your father through the gospel.
> 1 Corinthians 4:15 (NIV)

A FATHERLESS GENERATION

We too, are a generation without spiritual fathers and as a result, we are a generation without disciples.

Perhaps one of the reasons that we have increasing levels of converts and church attendees with decreasing numbers of committed disciples is because we fail to grasp the significance of the honor it is to be invited to follow Jesus.

Perhaps it is because we are content with our feeble attempts to modify our behavior on our own and do not grasp or believe that He alone has the power to lead us into the change that we desperately long for.

Or perhaps it is something different. Maybe it is the result of generations that have failed to carefully study the rabbi and his methods for themselves. Instead of passing the wisdom of the rabbi to our generation, they have only been able to pass on the wisdom of man.

The results of the wisdom of man surround us.

Attempts over the past generation to begin new churches by launching large primarily through methods of attraction where everything is focused on a Sunday morning event have failed to produce a generation that reflects Christ. Further efforts to transform the world through good deeds apart from the central truths of the gospel have produced moralistic campaigns that have served as little more than band-aids and aspirin rather than heart transplants. Efforts to centralize and elevate the Gospel apart from Christ's invitation to become His disciple have often unintentionally sent the message that Jesus exists to save us and meet our needs without recognizing that we were created to serve God and not the other way around. The result is often a self-centered salvation that becomes subtly focused on Jesus meeting our needs and the benefits of transformation rather than a Christ-centered existence focused on dying to self and reflecting Christ alone for His benefit and His glory.

34. Christ-centered.

Discipleship begins and ends with a rabbi and the invitation to follow the rabbi with the desire to become an imitation of the rabbi in every way. Christ-centered discipleship begins and ends with Jesus and the invitation to reflect Him through every area of our life.

Discipleship is not a whim.

It's not one option among many.

For those who call themselves Christians, Christ-centered discipleship is the invitation of Christ to follow Him in order to become His reflection.

It is the invitation to replace our thoughts with His thoughts, our actions with his actions, and our will with His will.

It is the invitation to respond.

Reflection

1. What ideas or images stood out to you in this book?

2. What was refreshing? Why?

3. What was frustrating? Why?

4. What questions do you have?

CHAPTER 2

LONGING FOR CHANGE

There is something else that is distinctive about the invitation the fishermen received from the rabbi as He walked along the shore of the sea of Galilee that probably contributed to their quick and immediate response. Rabbis didn't normally extend invitations to follow them. Rather, it was the responsibility of a potential disciple to seek a rabbi and to make a request similar to what many of us experience applying for college or for a job.

In fact, what made Christ's summons to the fishermen even more unique is that the invitations given by Jesus were to individuals who had already returned to the family business, implying that they had already been rejected by other rabbis. Remember, rabbis did not search for disciples. They waited for potential disciples to come to them.

Rabbis viewed their perspective on the words of God as sacred to the future of the people of Israel. It was up to a potential disciple to seek them out, and it was the rabbi's duty to protect the integrity of their legacy by only choosing disciples who would reflect the rabbi's life and teaching accurately.

If a rabbi rejected a potential disciple, it was because the rabbi did not think they were capable. They would instruct the individual to go home to the family business. There were no "do overs" or second chances. Once rejected, you were rejected by all of the rabbis. If one rabbi viewed you as incompetent or not capable, that was the label that your father had to explain to his friends when you showed up to work with him the next day.

Consider the scenario. A family has a son and raises him with the hope that perhaps one day a rabbi would consider him worthy enough to become a disciple. The boy grows and makes it through the entire education system and has one chance to apply for the opportunity to be a disciple, but is rejected by the rabbi. This means that boy is deemed not capable enough to someday imitate the rabbi accurately enough to reproduce their life and teaching into the lives of others. No other rabbi would allow themselves or their yoke of teaching to be degraded down to a second-rate option for a potential disciple. No other rabbi would stoop to accept the rejects of another rabbi, so the only option is for the youngster to return home to the family business filled with disappointment, rejection, and a mix of other emotions.

Imagine investing your entire life into the dream of becoming something only to be rejected. In one word, the person into whom you had placed all of your hopes and dreams for a better life labels you. Some of us do not need to imagine. We have been on the receiving end of rejection. Perhaps it was a relationship, or a career, or a dream that was crushed through rejection, injury, or simply the realization that we do not have what it takes to succeed. Someone or something labeled us and the label stuck.

This is where we meet the fishermen who were working with their father in the family business. Perhaps they were pulling in the nets, listening to Dad try to explain why his boys were back home. Or perhaps they had to put up with the know–it–all guy in the adjacent boat telling them that he had told them so and that at some point they should face the fact that they were fishermen and that is all they would ever be.

Then, the boys others considered incapable received an invitation from a rabbi who viewed them differently. Each of the Gospel writers record the immediacy of their response. They way left everything behind tells us that their hearts were longing for a change. But it wasn't just the fishermen, there were others too.

Consider Matthew, the tax collector, who at first glance would appear to be a success. Yet, he closed his books, left everything behind, and followed Christ.

> After this, Jesus went out and saw a tax collector by
> the name of Levi sitting at his tax booth. "Follow
> me," Jesus said to him, and Levi got up, left
> everything and followed him.
>
> Luke 5:27 (NIV)

Despite working under the label of tax collector, certainly Matthew had to be doing well for himself financially. Jewish tax collectors worked for the Roman government to ensure that Caesar received his portion of taxes. Not only would Matthew have had Roman soldiers to help collect the taxes, he would have had access also to the accounting books. As such, it's possible he had the opportunity to help himself to any excess collected. Jews despised tax collectors for betraying their people, serving the Roman government and receiving a profit. Even Jesus himself referred to tax collectors in the same category as pagan sinners, so it was not exactly a job that carried the same prestige as a rabbi's disciple.[1] (Matthew 18:17).

Prior to being labeled a tax collector, Matthew, who is also named as Levi (suggesting the probability of being of the priestly Levitical tribe). most likely had longed to be considered worthy of becoming the disciple of a rabbi as well. Matthew's understanding of the Old Testament as communicated through his Gospel demonstrates a higher level of education than merely sitting in the back row of a synagogue biding his time until he could become a tax collector.

40. Christ-centered.

Yet for some reason, prior to the invitation from Christ, he was not a disciple nor a priest, and so he had chosen to channel his energy and his longing for change into being a tax collector. I wonder if part of him didn't feel like he hadn't sold a piece of himself the day he collected his first tax from some underpaid Jewish father. I wonder if he felt he deserved it when his fellow Jews would talk behind his back with scorn. What is obvious is that he longed for change and did not think twice when given a rabbi's invitation to follow Him.

What about Simon? He is one of the disciples who managed to stay quietly in the background in spite of his flamboyant former affiliation prior to becoming one of Christ's disciples. Referred to in each of the four Gospels as Simon the Zealot, we can presume a lot about his desire for change.[2]

Even in modern terms, a zealot is described as a person who is fanatical and uncompromising in pursuit of their ideals. For Simon, it also meant an affiliation with a political movement to overthrow the Roman occupiers through violence. The Jewish historian Josephus tells us that the zealots were similar to the Pharisees in their approach to keeping the law, but did not think that mere piety would be enough to bring about the needed change.

Ironically, Matthew's decision to work for the Roman government and Simon's aspiration to overthrow the Roman government would have made them natural adversaries.

What about Andrew and his brother Simon Peter who were originally disciples of John the Baptist? Remember that this was a time when people were looking for the prophecy of Jeremiah to be fulfilled. People were watching and waiting for the deliverer to appear and to lead the people out from under Roman occupation and back into the blessing of God. Matthew chose the route of working for the government; Simon the Zealot chose the route of trying to overthrow the government; and John the Baptist became such a popular rabbi that the leaders in Jerusalem began to question if he was the messiah.

> Now this was John's testimony when the Jewish leaders in Jerusalem sent priests and Levites to ask him who he was. He did not fail to confess, but confessed freely, "I am not the Messiah."
> John 1:19-20 (NIV)

For disciples like Andrew, Philip, and Peter, this must have been an incredible declaration on behalf of John the Baptizer. They lived in an age where in an effort to enlarge their influence, anyone with even the hint of a following could claim to be the messiah and here was John not only saying that he was not, but claiming that their was another who was coming. John's harsh message of repentance and rebuke coupled with his hopeful testimony that Jesus was indeed the Messiah was all they needed to drop their nets and follow Christ.

It was not just men who were among the followers of Christ. The Gospels specifically list women too.

> After this, Jesus traveled about from one town and village to another, proclaiming the good news of the kingdom of God. The Twelve were with him, and also some women who had been cured of evil spirits and diseases: Mary (called Magdalene) from whom seven demons had come out; Joanna the wife of Chuza, the manager of Herod's household; Susanna; and many others. These women were helping to support them out of their own means.
>
> Luke 8:1-3 (NIV)

Consider the story of Mary Magdalene, a woman with a sketchy and painful past who would end up being first at the tomb of the risen Christ. Between possession by seven demons that had controlled her and her life selling herself to the abuse of men as a prostitute, she longed for change from shame, scorn, and judgment. No doubt in her demonically-crazed state she had been sold and abused by both Jewish and Roman alike, and here was a man, a rabbi, who thought of her as something different. He was someone who had not only healed her from demonic control, but a rabbi who considered her worthy to be in his presence. Certainly no rabbi had ever treated her that way before.

Mary, from Bethany, has a similar story. She took all the money she had, a year's wages, and used it to purchase perfume to anoint the feet of Christ prior to his entrance into Passion Week. Yet she was publically condemned by those who loved to appear religious on the outside but whose hearts were far from Christ.

> Six days before the Passover, Jesus arrived at Bethany, where Lazarus lived, whom Jesus had raised from the dead. Here a dinner was given in Jesus' honor. Martha served, while Lazarus was among those reclining at the table with him. Then Mary took about a pint of pure nard, an expensive perfume; she poured it on Jesus' feet and wiped his feet with her hair. And the house was filled with the fragrance of the perfume.

> But one of his disciples, Judas Iscariot, who was later to betray him, objected, "Why wasn't this perfume sold and the money given to the poor? It was worth a year's wages."

> John 12:1-6 (NIV)

On the opposite extreme was Joanna, wife of Chuza, the manager of Herod's household. She faced scorn of a different kind. Her husband was successful, powerful, and wealthy. From the perspective of the world, like Matthew it would seem that she had anything that she wanted (at least that money could buy). But she felt emptiness inside, and she knew something was missing

Each of these followers of Christ longed for change. Each one had a story in which they sought alternatives to the truth of Christ. Each one experienced longing for change to the point that they were willing to drop everything and become Christ's disciples. Each had a label—fisherman, tax collector, zealot, prostitute, trophy wife—that acted as a lens through which the world viewed them. Each encountered a Christ who saw them differently.

What about you?

- What are you longing for?

- What label do you desire to shed?

- What have you sought after hoping it would fill the void inside?

- Have you experienced the frustration of wanting to change without experiencing the victory that you longed for?

The Promise of Change

It's interesting to note that there is a billion dollar market for those who sell the promise of change. Whether patches, pills, or stock tips, charlatans abound with the latest and greatest snake oil formulas promising transformation and a better life to those who are willing to pay.

Consider for a moment some common conventional approaches that promise change, transformation, and a better life if we only pursue them hard or long enough.

- Scholarship sells us the idea that if know enough then we can change.
- Moralism tells us if we can learn to modify our behavior then we can change.
- Idealism tells us that the legalistic acquisition of the right characteristics or fulfillment of the right list will produce the change we long for.
- Materialism informs us that the pursuit of things will produce happiness, fulfillment, and a better life.
- Politics sells us on the hope for change with the right candidate or party and group of zealous followers.

Most of these promises for transformation, fulfillment, and change are also based on a conventional understanding and measurement of success. For example, there is the concept that we are successful if we feel better and see results fast. Why else would everyone from Madison Avenue to your local church market our society with seven tips for quick fixes in everything from books and infomercials to small groups and sermons? To appeal to the masses we are willing to turn discipleship into a microwave dinner of reheated fast food, while all the while Christ is inviting us to enjoy a slow-cooked meal from a crock pot.

Spiritual formation is not about the redemption of our actions or our feelings; it is about the transformation of our hearts. Are we really any different from the people of Jesus' day who sought money, politics, pleasure, and religious piety? Consider the lengths we will go in hopes of experiencing spiritual growth.

We seek after revival with the belief that it will change our hearts and transform our communities. Yet we are unaware of the historic ramifications areas such as The Burnt Over District in the early 19th century, an area in Northeast New York that continually sought revival and emotional conversions without implementing a systematic process of discipleship. The result of failing to ground people in doctrinal truth while continually seeking emotional experiences was the birthing of every type of cult imaginable, including but not limited to:

- The Mormons, who teach that Jesus is the half-brother of Lucifer.
- The Millerites, who preached that Christ would return on October 22,1844 and are the precursors to the Seventh Day Adventists.
- The Fox sisters, who started the American Spiritualism movement and practiced séances and communion with the dead.
- The Shakers, who were known for some unique beliefs and practices. For example, Shakers believed that God is both male and female. Anyone who joined their community was expected to remain celibate. In addition, they believed that while Jesus was the male manifestation of Christ, that Mother

Ann, who was the daughter of an English blacksmith, was the female version of the Incarnation.

- Last but certainly not least, the Oneida Society, which believed in free love and group marriage to the point that exclusive sexual relationships were frowned upon as being too possessive.

The irony is that each of these claimed to be followers of Jesus. As Paul wrote to the church in Corinth concerned because of the lack of true discipleship, we must ask the question: "What Jesus?"

> But I am afraid that just as Eve was deceived by the serpent's cunning, your minds may somehow be led astray from your sincere and pure devotion to Christ. For if someone comes to you and preaches a Jesus other than the Jesus we preached, or if you receive a different spirit from the Spirit you received, or a different gospel from the one you accepted, you put up with it easily enough.
>
> 2 Corinthians 11:3-4 (NIV)

In spite of all our sincerity it is easy to stray off track. Another way we go astray from God's plan is when we pursue religious involvement thinking that finding the right program and getting more people involved will result in greater personal holiness. However, the harsh reality is that busy does not equal holy. Most of the time it simply results in exhaustion.

It is the same with small groups. Years ago, we were told that if people get involved outside of Sunday mornings in small group Bible studies that it will result in transformation and change. Has it worked?

What about worship? Has the renewed emphasis on worship for the past twenty years brought about the promised transformation and change we desire?

What if we re-emphasize preaching? We can preach longer sermons and make them available on podcasts for download. Will this result in transformation and change? If not, perhaps we just have not recommitted ourselves to Christ enough?

Or we are simply not trying hard enough to read our Bibles and pray? Or perhaps we need to take another long survey that will help us reflect on what program we need to implement in order to get more people engaged?

It is not that any of these things are bad in and of themselves. When we confuse the process of being a disciple with the product of spiritual maturity, then we wrongly celebrate the process rather than aiming for the product. We end up focusing on activities and programs rather than on Christ.

In our efforts to develop the perfect program we sometimes wrongly assume God is lucky finally have us on His team, that He is breathing a sigh of relief that we are here to help Him. But one thing is abundantly clear from Scripture: God, not our programs, is the cause of spiritual growth.

> I planted the seed, Apollos watered it, but God has been making it grow.
>
> 1 Corinthians 3:6 (NIV)

> So neither the one who plants nor the one who waters is anything, but only God, who makes things grow.
>
> 1 Corinthians 3:7 (NIV)

Pauls's words to the Corinthian church make it clear that while God chooses to allow us to be part of the process, He is ultimately the only cause for spiritual growth. Paul emphasizes this point further when he reminds the church in Colossus of the centrality of Christ in the process of God's plan for growth.

> They have lost connection with the head, from whom the whole body, supported and held together by its ligaments and sinews, grows as God causes it to grow.
>
> Colossians 2:19 (NIV)

There is no magic speaker who will usher in lasting transformation, no program that will introduce lasting change, and no magic book describing how to experience God and a life of happier Mondays that actually works. Growth comes from God alone through Christ alone.

50. Christ-centered.

Until we stop viewing Christ only as creator and redeemer and start understanding him also as our rabbi, we will continue our insane attempts to help Him out.

So, how do we uncover God's plan? Is it ours to uncover, or is it one of those unfathomable mysteries where God chooses to keep us in the dark?

This question introduces another theory. Perhaps we are trying too hard. Perhaps our emphasis on growth is not actually God's plan. Perhaps what He really desires is to keep spiritual growth a mystery. It's kind of like His personal secret where He holds all the cards. The Holy Spirit comes and goes, organically transforming wherever it pleases, and if we just happen to be lucky enough for it to impact our lives, then we are one of the blessed ones. Perhaps we are just supposed to "let go and let God."

But letting go and letting God is not found in the Bible, and it is not a biblical foundation for the process of sanctification.

In the same letter to Colossae, just a few verses earlier, Paul answers by reminding the church not only of the centrality of Christ, but of His promise that we will have full understanding through Him.

> My goal is that they may be encouraged in heart and united in love, so that they may have the full riches of complete understanding, in order that they may know the mystery of God, namely, Christ, in whom are hidden all the treasures of wisdom and knowledge.
>
> Colossians 2:2-3 (NIV)

According to these verses, God does not want to frustrate us, but to encourage us toward our complete understanding of Him through Christ. The mysterious treasures of God, including all wisdom and knowledge, are found in Christ. In other words, we are in the same position of viewing Christ as our rabbi as were the original disciples. If we want spiritual growth, we must look deeply into the person of Christ.

A few verses later, in verse eight of the second chapter, Paul warns that in contrast to those who look deeply into Christ to find their answers, some will look to human traditions and will create philosophies that are not only hollow but will imprison people.

> See to it that no one takes you captive through hollow and deceptive philosophy, which depends on human tradition and the elemental spiritual forces of this world rather than on Christ.
>
> Colossians 2:8

If that is not a description of some of our modern discipleship methods and attempts, then I do not know what is. We are surrounded by the results of this warning.

As individuals and organizations, we have attempted to create spiritual growth programs and tools that have led people into the captivity of moralistic, legalistic religious systems rather than on Christ alone. As a result, we have missed the invitation of discipleship and the desired outcome of reflecting Christ.

Our collective best efforts to create programs for discipleship that transforms lives have failed.

I remember fifteen years ago, when I attempted to sell a new program to my junior and senior high students. There was a national conference that broadcasted itself as day one of a global transformative movement of students. It was the event that would be the beginning of all other events. It had the best speakers and the best bands and it was in the largest stadium that could be found. The marketing was phenomenal. In addition to tee shirts and posters there was a promotional video that I played for our group as I announced the event. But instead of cheers and accolades resulting in kids begging to participate, I was met with the cynical gaze of a teenager. With insight beyond her years, she responded by saying, "Not every event can be bigger and better than the one before it. Eventually, someone needs to wise up, stop trying to sell us stuff, and just help us make sense of how we are supposed to follow Jesus."

She was right. At some point we need to wise up and realize that our programs and philosophies are not working, and we need to stop viewing Christ only as our

Creator and Redeemer and begin seeking to understand and embrace Him as our rabbi and recognize that our job is not to design another discipleship program but to uncover and communicate Christ's plan for making disciples.

CHAPTER 3

SECRETS IN THE SOIL

Throughout the New Testament there is a clear, repeated expectation that we grow in our Christian faith. For example, the Apostle Paul exhorted the church in Ephesus to "grow up" in their relationship with Christ:

> Then we will no longer be infants, tossed back and forth by the waves, and blown here and there by every wind of teaching and by the cunning and craftiness of people in their deceitful scheming. Instead, speaking the truth in love, we will grow to become in every respect the mature body of him who is the head, that is, Christ.
> Ephesians 4:14-15 (NIV)

Paul had similar prayers for both the church in Philippi and Thessalonica:

> And this is my prayer: that your love may abound more and more in knowledge and depth of insight.
> Philippians 1:9 (NIV)

> We ought always to give thanks to God for you, brothers, as is right, because your faith is growing abundantly, and the love of every one of you for one another is increasing.
> 2 Thessalonians 1:3 (ESV)

Another apostle and New Testament author, Peter, also emphasizes the necessity of growth:

> But grow in the grace and knowledge of our Lord and Savior Jesus Christ. To him be the glory both now and to the day of eternity. Amen.
> 2 Peter 3:18 (ESV)

> Like newborn babies, crave pure spiritual milk, so that by it you may grow up in your salvation.
> 2 Peter 2:2 (NIV)

The gospel writer John compares different stages of spiritual maturity to the stages of physical maturity:

> I am writing to you, fathers,
>   because you know him who is from the beginning.
> I am writing to you, young men,
>   because you have overcome the evil one.
> I write to you, dear children,

because you know the Father.
I write to you, fathers,
   because you know him who is from the beginning.
I write to you, young men,
   because you are strong,
   and the word of God lives in you,
   and you have overcome the evil one.
                                1 John 2:13-14 (NIV)

The author of Hebrews went so far as to not only chastise people that should have been further along in their spiritual growth, but to also make a reference to the concept brought up by Peter that different stages of growth benefit from different types of teaching to meet specific spiritual needs.

In fact, though by this time you ought to be teachers, you need someone to teach you the elementary truths of God's word all over again. You need milk, not solid food!
                                Hebrews 5:12 (NIV)

Most of us do not question whether or not we should be growing. Whether the feeling is from ourselves or from God, we feel the tension and frustration of that expectation. The real question is *how* are we supposed to grow? What does it look like? What should it feel like? What should we expect along the way? Is what we are experiencing normal? Once we have identified the desired outcome that spiritual maturity means becoming a reflection of Christ, the questions that really need to be answered to make sense of our lives include:

- Does Scripture identify a clear, Christ-centered path with distinct stages and specific, manageable steps for growing toward the desired outcome?

- Is it possible for us to identify from Scripture what is expected of us at each step in the process of transformation?

- Is it possible for us to identify from Scripture both our spiritual needs and our spiritual growth barriers in order to be equipped to get the help that we need and make sense of the journey?

- Is the whole process understandable and easy to apply or do we need to have a special degree in biblical languages in order to figure it out?

Not only does Jesus want to answer those questions for us, but implicit in the rabbinical invitation to follow Him is the promise that He will. I do not believe that Jesus wants to keep the answers to spiritual growth and transformation a secret. He simply desires for us to stop trying to create our own methodologies, humble ourselves, and ask Him for wisdom as we are instructed by James:

> If any of you lacks wisdom, you should ask God, who gives generously to all without finding fault, and it will be given to you.   James 1:5 (NIV)

58. Christ-centered.

In case we are wondering what exactly we should ask Him to give us wisdom about, let's start with asking if we truly believe it is the will of God that we experience spiritual growth and transform into His reflection. Because if we do, then we have an awesome prayer from Paul for the church in Colossae:

> For this reason, since the day we heard about you, we have not stopped praying for you. We continually ask God to fill you with the knowledge of his will through all the wisdom and understanding that the Spirit gives.
>
> Colossians 1:9 (NIV)

It is similar to the promise made to the nation of Israel through the prophet Jeremiah:

> You will seek me and find me when you seek me with all your heart.
>
> Jeremiah 29:13 (NIV)

A prayer that I found myself praying many times during my personal search was:

> "God, I believe You desire for us to become reflections of Yours. Quite frankly, I have tried everything I know and still have no idea exactly how that is supposed to happen. You promised to fill us with the knowledge of Your will, with all of the wisdom and understanding that comes from Your Spirit. I'm humbling myself, asking for Your wisdom, and holding You to Your promise that You will give

generously without finding fault. So I am thanking You in advance for keeping your promise."

"But," some of us are thinking to ourselves, "I've prayed that prayer not once, but a thousand times. That prayer is nice, but it sounds too simplistic. It feels too much like a formula. I've tried it, and it did not work for me." For those who are in that spot, my heart goes out to you. I've been there. Take encouragement from the words of Paul:

> Let us not become weary in doing good, for at the proper time we will reap a harvest if we do not give up.
> Galatians 6:9

And for the sake of further clarity, it is also important to note that while I have come to believe that the answers that we are looking for are actually quite easy to identify, once we understand what we are looking for, it took me over twelve years of intentional searching back and forth throughout the Scriptures to making the connections.

APPROACHING OUR RABBI

One of my biggest breakthroughs came when I stopped approaching Jesus through the eyes of a pastor and began to understand Him from the perspective of a rabbi. Over and over again throughout the Gospels we see and hear Jesus operating and teaching from the perspective of a Jewish rabbi. It is the responsibility of a rabbi to model the process of transformation as well as the product of discipleship, because the rabbinical goal for each of their disciples is that their disciples would not only reflect their life, but would repeat their process while making future disciples.

Christ takes responsibility for our transformation when He says, "I will make you."[1] That is a promise that is still as applicable today as it was with His original disciples. He has not stopped making disciples. This means we can stop trying to create programs to disciple people and instead put our efforts into uncovering, understanding, and clearly communicating Christ's process for making disciples. When we fail to recognize Christ at the center of the process of transformation, we end up participating in moralistic or religious attempts to modify behavior through disciplines that are powered by our own self-will and end up being nothing more than self-indulgent religious activities. Without the presence of Christ and the power of the Spirit of God at the center of our transformation our desire for change can actually becomes an idol in and of itself. When this happens it is possible for following Christ to become self-centered and self-serving instead of Christ-centered and Christ serving.

The reality of Christ-centered discipleship is possibly very different than most of us have experienced in our modern culture of self-centered discipleship. Books, sermons, and seminars sell promises to make just about every part of our life more comfortable or desirable. Promises to satisfy our longing for change through the practice of increased effort or discipline are seldom fruitful, and yet transformation is the promise for everyone who desires to become an imitator of Christ. Many of us we will need to begin with the question: What will I need to unlearn regarding conventional approaches to spiritual formation I've acquired over the years so that I can participate in a Christ-centered approach?

Shortly after presenting the rabbinical yoke of His teaching to His new disciples, Jesus told a parable that is recorded in three of the four Gospels. While telling parables was a normal part of the teaching style of a rabbi, there is something abnormal about the way this particular parable is recorded for us. It is one of only a few of all of the parables of Christ that is not left open to interpretation. Each of the three accounts by Matthew, Mark, and Luke all include a detailed interpretation and explanation of the parable by Christ for His new disciples.

THE HINT METHOD

Jesus begins the parable using a common rabbinical technique call the *remez* or, "hint method," in which He makes a vague reference to a specific passage in the Old Testament in order to inform His disciples that He is going to expand on the meaning of something previously revealed by God. Central to the hint method was the rabbi's expectation that his disciples have a strong knowledge and grasp of the Old Testament. The rabbi would reveal a new or deeper meaning or interpretation that would be coupled with a secret or key that they could understand and apply to their immediate lives.

62. Christ-centered.

This particular parable is important enough that Jesus begins with several hints to ensure that both the disciples that are there with Him are tracking as well as those of us following him over two thousand years later. The first two hints given by Christ are subtle, especially for those of us with Gentile ears and who are unfamiliar with the teaching style and not as thoroughly schooled in the Old Testament. In Mark 4:3, Jesus begins his parable with these words:

"Listen! A farmer went out to sow his seed."

You and I most likely think, "Ok, Jesus is going to tell us a story about a farmer." However, the disciples who were hearing these words from Christ recognized two vague hints to a passage in Isaiah 28 that begins with similar words and informs us of the wisdom God gives a farmer. Immediately they began tracking with Christ as He continues with the parable. In case, like me, you don't happen to have the passage in Isaiah already memorized like the disciples most likely did, it is helpful to read it and understand the context. Pay close attention to the hint in verse twenty three, and highlight or underline any parts that anticipate the fact that Jesus is going to expand on this passage with *remez* (secret keys) for you to apply to your life.

Listen and hear my voice;
pay attention and hear what I say.

When a farmer plows for planting, does he plow
continually?
    Does he keep on breaking up and working the soil?
When he has leveled the surface,
    does he not sow caraway and scatter cumin?
Does he not plant wheat in its place,
    barley in its plot,
    and spelt in its field?
His God instructs him
    and teaches him the right way.
Caraway is not threshed with a sledge,
    nor is the wheel of a cart rolled over cumin;
caraway is beaten out with a rod,
    and cumin with a stick.
Grain must be ground to make bread;
    so one does not go on threshing it forever.
The wheels of a threshing cart may be rolled over it,
    but one does not use horses to grind grain.
All this also comes from the Lord Almighty,
    whose plan is wonderful,
    whose wisdom is magnificent.

                                            Isaiah 28:23-29

SECRETS IN THE SOIL

In case you are not from a farming background,
these six verses are pretty cool. Twice in six verses we
learn that God gives farmers insight to differentiate what
is done in the soil to maximize their harvest. The word
"differentiate" is not one I was familiar with a few years
ago prior to making a career change from being a pastor
to a full-time teacher, but it is a common word in
classroom instruction. To differentiate is to recognize the
differences in how individual students learn and to

change the instructional approach to meet the different learning need or to overcome the unique obstacles to learning for individual students. The goal is to meet needs and remove obstacle to ensure each individual student has the maximum opportunity to learn and grow. The alternative to differentiation is for teachers to treat every student the same while failing to recognize their unique differences.

God, through the prophet Isaiah, informs us that it would be foolish for farmers to treat all of the soil the same while simply trying harder to produce a harvest. Instead, through wisdom acquired by God Himself, they have learned to recognize seasons and stages in the soil that allows them to differentiate to different needs and avoid obstacles that would keep them from maximizing their harvest.

It is in light of and in reference to this passage that Jesus then tells a parable about a farmer who sows seed into diverse types of soil and receives four different types of results. You can almost imagine the disciples thinking to themselves that they are tracking with their rabbi as they search for His hidden meaning and the key to what He desires for them to apply to their lives.

Mark mentions that they waited until He was alone to ask Him what He was talking about. Then Jesus explains the meaning of the parable to His disciples by saying that each of the elements within the story illustrates specific things. The seed scattered by the farmer represents the Word of God. The soil represents our hearts and the different ways our hearts receive and respond to the Word of God. As Jesus profiles each type of soil, He refers to the last as good soil, and He tells us the good soil bears much fruit. Jesus instructs us that one of the key characteristics of a heart that is represented by the image of good soil is that it hears, understands, and responds to the Word of God.

> But the seed falling on good soil refers to someone who hears the word and understands it. This is the one who produces a crop, yielding a hundred, sixty or thirty times what was sown.
>
> Matthew 13:23 (NIV)

The word translated into our English Bibles as "understand" is from the Greek word *suniemi*, which is commonly translated to mean, "to understand or comprehend." In context, the word literally means, "to bring things together mentally in a way that assembles individual facts into an organized whole and makes sense of them."

Remember, Jesus' goal for His disciples is to transform them into His reflections. To accomplish this He must not only model for them the process of transformation in their own lives, but also model for them the methods He desires for them to imitate as they reproduce His process in the lives of those who follow. Prior to giving this parable, He had just completed giving them His yoke of expectations through His Sermon on the Mount. He had already sent them on their first practice trip to teach and spread the Gospel, and He was helping them learn how to "make sense of" or how to differentiate the hearts of their hearers for maximum effectiveness.

In other words, Jesus is trying to get fishermen and tax collectors to think like farmers in order that they can apply the wisdom of God to the process of spreading the word of God. If you are still a bit confused, that's okay. You are in good company. The disciples needed a bit more of an explanation to understand it for themselves. Watch how Christ explains it:

> Then Jesus said to them, "Don't you understand this parable? How then will you understand any parable? The farmer sows the word. Some people are like seed along the path, where the word is sown. As soon as they hear it, Satan comes and takes away the word that was sown in them. Others, like seed sown on rocky places, hear the word and at once receive it with joy. But since they have no root, they last only a short time. When trouble or persecution comes because of the word, they quickly fall away. Still others, like seed sown among thorns, hear the word; but the worries of this life, the deceitfulness of wealth and the desires for other things come in and choke the word, making it unfruitful.
> Others, like seed sown on good soil, hear the word, accept it, and produce a crop—some thirty, some sixty, some a hundred times what was sown."
>
> Mark 4:13-20 (NIV)

Invest some time and read the way Matthew and Luke record the explanation of Christ in their Gospels as well. Both add unique insights and imagery. When we combine the three passages, they paint a fuller picture. You can find the full passages in Matthew 13:1-23 and Luke 8:1-15. Both also include two additional, blatant *remez* or hints back to the book of Isaiah.

Remember that the rabbinical expectation of the *remez* is that there is both an expansion of a previous revelation of God and a deeper truth being revealed that requires close examination on behalf of the disciple.

FROM FISHERMEN TO FARMERS

Christ used the parable to explain that our hearts are like soil farmers have to work with. Each one is a different field. Some are hard as a paved path, and the Word of God never has a chance to penetrate because the heart is not ready to receive it. Others are full of rocks or weeds, and they react accordingly. Some hearts are full of rich soil, and they receive the Word of God ready to hear it and to respond with understanding.

Isaiah also informs us that God gives wisdom to the farmers to work in the soil and not simply give up or treat all of it the same. God instructs the farmer and teaches him how to differentiate to meet individual needs and overcome obstacles that hinder the maximum yield or harvest that a field can produce.

What does Christ desire to produce in our lives through our receiving, understanding, and responding to the word of God? A harvest. What type of harvest? Listen to the words of the writer of Hebrews and of Paul as they answer that question:

68. Christ-centered.

They disciplined us for a little while as they thought best; but God disciplines us for our good, in order that we may share in his holiness. No discipline seems pleasant at the time, but painful. Later on, however, it produces a harvest of righteousness and peace for those who have been trained by it.

Hebrews 12:10-11 (NIV)

Now he who supplies seed to the sower and bread for food will also supply and increase your store of seed and will enlarge the harvest of your righteousness.

2 Corinthians 9:10 (NIV)

Want to know something awesome? The word, "discipline," is the root for the word, "discipleship." Jesus is giving His disciples a way to evaluate their hearts in order to recognize their spiritual needs and obstacles to growth that stand in the way of understanding and responding to the word of God and seeing Him produce a harvest of righteousness in their lives.

He gave His disciples His yoke, and then He gave them what they needed in order to walk with the wisdom of the farmer.

He gave them the opportunity to stop the insanity of trying harder and to avoid the religious attempts to please God through their own efforts and He invited them to allow Him to produce a harvest of righteousness in and through their lives.

And His invitation to those who have ears to hear is still valid for you and me today.

Reflection

1. What ideas or images stood out to you in this book?

2. What was refreshing? Why?

3. What was frustrating? Why?

4. What questions do you have?

70. Christ-centered.

CHAPTER 4

GOOD INTENTIONS
AND DIRTY LENSES

If things are not crystal clear yet, do not be concerned. For those of us who have not grown up in agricultural communities, it is difficult to appreciate how soil matters to a farmer. For a farmer whose living depends on the health of the soil in their field, soil is the life and heartbeat of their existence. Good soil must be cared for in order to ensure the maximum yield during a harvest. Good soil: good harvest. Bad soil: no harvest.

My family had the opportunity to observe a farmer up close for a few years when our yard backed up to a 600-acre farm. It was pretty cool to watch all the different times the farmer would pass through the soil during the year to ensure that the right things were happening at the right time.

The intent of Christ's parable was not to present a story about soil that would leave us better informed with a list of facts about hearts and how they receive the word of God. The point of any parable using the *remez* method was always for the disciple to discover, understand, and apply a deeper truth or the key of the parable to their immediate life in a transformational way.

First, a parable was designed to stir a level of curiosity in the disciples that would quicken their hunger to study the Word of God to discover the deeper meaning for themselves. Then the parable was designed to create a new level of insight and understanding in the life of the disciple that would result in fruit as it was applied.

Christ lays out his rabbinical yoke for what his disciples were to believe and how they were to behave through His Sermon on the Mount. After the Sermon on the Mount, Christ presents the framework for different stages of growth, including different spiritual needs and obstacles to growth at each stage in the process. As such, we should not be surprised to find either of these key teachings at the front end of His ministry, because the rabbinical way would be for Him to model and expand upon both His yoke of beliefs and behaviors as well as His yoke for understanding and application throughout the rest of His ministry. Moreover, we should expect His disciples to communicate and repeat His framework through their teaching in a way that is clear and easy to understand, because His expectation was for them to not only apply it to their own lives but also to reproduce it into the lives of future disciples.

What's cool is that they do. Throughout the rest of the New Testament, each of the writers identify different stages of growth that follow the same pattern presented in the parable of the sower and the seed. In addition, each one also continues to add clarity to the profile of each stage in the process, as well as show spiritual needs and obstacles to growth that disciples and disciple-makers need to be aware of to experience personal transformation and increased effectiveness.

There is one other expectation that must be met in order for us to truly embrace the idea that Christ is presenting more than just a simple story about dirt. Not only do His disciples need to teach the process, but we need to see if and how Christ teaches and applies these principles throughout the rest of His ministry.

At that point in my personal journey of searching Scripture for Christ's process, I was convinced Christ's complete model for making disciples must be clearly expressed beyond just a single parable. However, numerous times reading through the Gospels had yet to uncover anything. The only option I had left was to systematically dissect every one of Christ's conversations recorded in the Gospels. The problem was that this was going to take a lot of time. Time that I did not have by myself.

12 FRESHMEN

God chose to use twelve freshmen in high school to uncover the key that would unlock the next step. It was the fourth quarter of their freshman year, and I was looking for a way to authentically help them put into practice Bible study skills they had learned throughout the previous three quarters. What happened next seemed like a win-win scenario for both my students and myself. They would have a valid project and I would have twelve captive teaching assistants. Over the course of the next several weeks of the quarter, they would examine each and every one of the conversations of Christ to learn whether or not He revealed the key to His process of discipleship.

Each student had a laptop computer and a spreadsheet, and together they were assigned to examine a dozen Bible translations. Beginning with the verse, "Follow me, and I will make you fishers of men,"[1] they were to identify and examine every conversation Jesus had with anyone in the Gospels that included the word "follow."

After pinpointing each of the conversations, they were to do a context Bible study and note who Jesus was having the conversation with, what was the response of that individual or group of people, and what happened immediately before and after each of the conversations. Then they were to cross-reference the occurrence and note whether this was an isolated or unique incident or if

74. Christ-centered.

it was an expansion of an event was recorded in another Gospel as well.

When the students finished this part of the assignment, they observed that there seemed to be a distinction between the audience who received Christ's invitation to follow him and those who received a slightly different invitation to deny themselves and follow him.

Then a student wondered out loud to the group, based on the differences in context between the situations, if they were actually looking at two different invitations rather than a single invitation that was worded differently. Another student added to that question by wondering if there were other invitations that could be identified in the Gospels.

With no agenda, no background in the Greek language, and nothing to gain other than the intrigue of discovering God's revelation from God's word, these twelve students began to sort through and examine every conversation of Christ recorded in the Gospels. Pretty soon something amazing began to appear.

Perhaps it is because God enjoys using the foolish things of the world to confound the wise[2] Or perhaps simply to ensure that no one would receive credit for the discovery but the author Himself, a series of seven distinct invitations began to emerge from the text.

The Invitations of Christ

What made these invitations so intriguing and so difficult to find through a straight devotional reading of the text is that they are not presented in a list. As the students excitedly circled their chairs and laptops around a giant whiteboard to compare notes, they discovered that although in a casual reading of the text each invitation appears to be random, when the seven invitations are strung together they form a sort of path or process toward spiritual maturity that invites people to move away from self-will and pride toward reflecting Christ.

The students found that Jesus invites us to repent, believe, follow, love, deny, go, and teach. There are a couple reasons we decided the words should be called invitations and not commands. One of the main reasons is because the word "command" implies that Christ is ordering people to do something. He isn't. He is inviting them and giving them the opportunity to respond. Everyone responds; some positively, others negatively.

Here is a brief overview of the invitations and their context:

Repent.

Repent means to "change your mind." Christ invites people to change their mind about how they view Him and who they think He is. While at first glance the invitation appears to be used multiple times, closer examination reveals the invitation is used only three unique times by itself. Christ always gives the call to repent to individuals or groups of people who are skeptical of Him and His ministry.

BELIEVE.

Sometimes repent and believe are used in the same invitation. Other times, the Apostle John uses the words "believe" and "faith" interchangeably, but in every instance it is an invitation for people who are seeking Christ to put their faith in Him.

FOLLOW.

The invitation to follow is a rabbinical invitation that indicates a rabbi believes the potential disciple has what it takes to become their imitator. This invitation is always given to those whose hearts are already bent toward belief in Jesus except for two distinct times. Close examination of these passages, however, reveals that Christ is using the invitation to follow Him as a direct way of showing them their need to repent and change their mind about how they view him and what they are placing their faith in.

LOVE AND DENY.

What makes the next set of invitations unique is

that the calls to love and to deny are only ever given to disciples of Christ's who are already informed of His yoke. These disciples are then given the invitation to love Christ and deny themselves, or to love themselves and deny Christ. Understanding this brings added insight into the parable of the sower when we parallel it to the heart that struggles with the weeds. In the parable, Christ specifically identifies the weeds to be the financial stress and the worries of this life. These are two things that both have the ability to remove our focus from Christ and choke our growth.

GO AND TEACH.

Finally, the last set of invitations fittingly appear at the very end of the gospels when the disciples reached the stage where they could imitate and reproduce Christ not just as followers, but as friends and fellow disciple makers.

I encourage you to use an online Bible program to check the validity of what these teens discovered for yourself. Begin with basic word studies and then examine the context of each passage. I've led groups of pastors, teachers, and students around the world through this activity. It is continually fascinating to watch as God's word comes to life through the exercise.

PUTTING THE PIECES TOGETHER

What can we learn and apply from the invitations of Christ, and how do they fit together with the parable of the sower?

Christ used the invitations as assessment tools to examine the hearts of the people He was speaking to; to differentiate His teaching to meet their needs and to challenge them to overcome their obstacles to growth.

ASSESSING OUR HEARTS

Christ taught that our hearts are like soil. Sometimes soil is hard and dry. Other times it is rich and receptive. Sometimes it is rocky and rootless, while other times it is infested with weeds. The reality is that soil, like our hearts, continually changes and must be carefully tended.

Discipleship is not like a baseball diamond where we run to first, get into scoring position on second, steal third, and then make it home off of a sacrifice pop fly deep into center field and return to the dug-out impressed with ourselves for rounding the bases and scoring a run for Jesus.

Discipleship is the tending of our hearts during the transformational process of learning to change our mind about who Christ is. It is placing our belief in Him alone as both our Savior and Lord in every area of our life as we learn to follow Him and apply His teaching to our lives. Discipleship is realizing that the trials of life are

God's opportunity to teach us perseverance and grow in maturity as we learn to follow His example in the Garden of Gethsemane by denying ourselves and wholeheartedly obeying His will out of hearts that have learned to trust him and have grown in love for him. Discipleship is making the most of every opportunity to go and share with others what God is teaching us, and teaching them to apply the invitations to their lives so their hearts can be changed, too.

Discipleship is recognizing that our hearts are invited constantly to participate in Christ's process of transforming every part of us into His reflection. It is recognizing our need for accurate self-assessment in order to understand how to address our specific spiritual needs and overcome our unique spiritual obstacles based on the soil of our hearts. This is not so we can wallow in our present circumstances, but so that our hearts can receive the word of God with understanding and will bear the fruit of continual transformation.

Christ used His invitations to assess how individuals would respond to Him as the Word of God. Christ used the parable of the soil to outline to His disciples how they could use the wisdom of God to maximize their understanding of the various stages, needs, and obstacles that are found in the soil of our hearts. But that information is worthless unless we have a way to examine our hearts.

EXAMINE YOURSELVES

Throughout Scripture we are instructed to examine our lives as a regular part of the process of spiritual growth. For example, we are charged by Paul to scrutinize our lives every time that we take communion:

> Everyone ought to examine themselves before they eat of the bread and drink from the cup.
>
> 1 Corinthians 11:28 (NIV)

We are also instructed to examine and test ourselves to see if we are in the faith.

> Examine yourselves, to see whether you are in the faith. Test yourselves. Or do you not realize this about yourselves, that Jesus Christ is in you? - unless indeed you fail to meet the test!
>
> 2 Corinthians 13:5 (ESV)

WHAT EXACTLY ARE WE EXAMINING?

I remember sitting in church as a high school student and laughing quietly to myself each time the pastor read those words. I would quietly search my arms in mock inspection. What exactly did he mean by examine myself? What was I looking for? How would I know if I found it? I also found it ironic that it often seemed like only a few seconds would pass between when the pastor would direct us to examine ourselves and when it was time to participate in communion by eating and drinking.

It always seemed like a fairly quick examination process. What would have happened if someone actually found something, assuming they knew what they were looking for? If we found we had done something wrong, would a quick apology have sufficed? Were we supposed to jump up in repentance? There was hardly time for my mock examination of my arms; certainly there wouldn't have been time for me to run across the auditorium to apologize to a person who I had wronged or to work out some personal repentance issues between me and God. It's not like they would have stopped the service for that – would they?

The theological irony is that our attempts at self-examination are futile at best anyway. Scripture is pretty clear in Jeremiah 17:9 that our hearts are deceitful, unknowable, and desperately wicked, so how could any self-examination be accurate without deceiving myself into thinking that I'm a good person?

Wait a minute! Perhaps that is why the pastor never gave us time for a true examination! Because we would all be lying to ourselves anyway (and because he was just trying to keep the whole service under an hour so we could make it to the restaurants before the churches down the street let out and we would have to stand in line).

How exactly are we supposed to examine our hearts and apply Christ's teaching of the parable of the sower and the seed when we can't trust our own hearts to perform the examination and we are commanded not to judge someone else?[3]

What standard exists for sinful people like us to use when we can't trust our own internal judgment?

What option is available to us that can penetrate our hearts and identify how we respond to the Word of God when we can never be sure that our personal examination is accurate?

We could compare ourselves to others in an effort to gauge our maturity against theirs, but Paul also warns us against that when he writes:

> Not that we dare to classify or compare ourselves with some of those who are commending themselves. But when they measure themselves by one another and compare themselves with one another, they are without understanding.
> 2 Corinthians 10:12 (ESV)

So we should neither judge ourselves from the perspective of our own inaccurate and deceptive hearts, nor should we foolishly compare ourselves against others. So how could Paul instruct us to do something that is impossible in and of ourselves?

Many of us have participated in a communion service and have found ourselves wondering something similar in the past: How am I supposed to examine myself with good intentions but dirty lenses? For some, the realization that our self-examination is tainted by our own sin has been the cause of a spirit of unrest, discomfort, frustration, or even cynicism or anger toward ourselves, the communion service, and often even toward God Himself.

In our conversations with God and our private thoughts, we admit we struggle spiritually and that we desire to accurately examine the soil of our hearts, but we have no idea how. We have bartered with God and hoped He would respond with writing on the wall or that the Bible will magically open itself to a verse that held an answer or direction for us to follow.

When those options have failed, we recommitted ourselves to trying harder, and for a while our self-willed attempts numbed the pain in our souls. Eventually spiritual exhaustion caught up with us and we stopped asking for help or trying to understand.

Some of us have wrestled with bitterness towards ourselves, thinking that everyone else seems happy or content with their spiritual growth so the problem must be ours alone. Perhaps there was something about ourselves that God found unworthy of His secrets. Others of us have grown bitter toward God, wondering what we might have done to Him. Could He not see that we wanted to grow? Yet, the answers we desired simply were not available to us in an understandable way.

But Jesus does not desire to tease us or to without His plan for our transformation. As our rabbi, He outlines His path and gives us His invitation to not only accurately examine ourselves by responding to the Word of God, but to allow the Word of God to inform and equip us with direction and the fruit that accompanies identifying our spiritual needs and obstacles to growth and understanding our next steps. The Bible says that,

> "The LORD sees not as man sees: man looks on the outward appearance, but the LORD looks on the heart."
>
> 1 Samuel 16:7b (ESV)

The truth is that outward actions and behaviors can be deceiving. Knowing this, Jesus directed us to look beneath the surface of exterior actions and behaviors in order to get an accurate measurement when He said in John 7:24, "Look beneath the surface so you can judge correctly" (NLT) But where do we look and how can we make an accurate assessment to see ourselves as He see us?

Reflection

1. What ideas or images stood out to you in this book?

2. What was refreshing? Why?

3. What was frustrating? Why?

4. What questions do you have?

86. Christ-centered.

CHAPTER 5

EXAMINE YOUR REFLECTION

The one thing in the world that promises to not only look beneath the surface to accurately judge our hearts but also has the power to equip us for our next steps in the process of spiritual maturity is the written Word of God.

> For the word of God is living and active and sharper than any two-edged sword, and piercing as far as the division of soul and spirit, of both joints and marrow, and able to judge the thoughts and intentions of the heart.
>
> Hebrews 4:12 (NASB).

Unlike our own attempts to judge the attitudes of our heart that are tainted by our own sin, the Word of God promises to penetrate like a two-edged sword.

At the time that verse was written, the two-edged Roman gladius was considered so sharp that it could slice through a hair that was succumbing to the gravitational pull of the earth. Even now, it takes a laser to separate the bone from the marrow inside. This is the promise of Scripture toward how it approaches the examination of our hearts.

But God does not say that His word will leave us open on an examination table without equipping us for what to do next; it also promises to show us our next step and to equip us to accomplish our purpose.

> All Scripture is God-breathed and is useful for teaching, rebuking, correcting and training in righteousness, so that the servant of God may be thoroughly equipped for every good work.
> 2 Timothy 3:16-17 (NIV)

God not only promises that His word will look beneath the surface of our life, but that it will equip us with understanding to take our next steps in our relationship with Him.

This chapter is your opportunity to invite the Holy Spirit to use God's Word to examine the soil of your heart and to equip you to understand how to respond to His invitations in your life.

In the chapter you will find the Words of God laid out in a simple, easy-to-read format with the invitation that you will read through God's word and simply highlight or underline the words, phrases, or verses that resonate with you and where you are at in your spiritual journey with Christ at this moment in time.

Don't be surprised if there are sections that do not seem to apply or if there are parts of numerous sections that seem to resonate with you. Trust God to use His word to examine your heart and to reveal Himself to you.

Before you begin the assessment, ask God to give you an understanding of what you read and invite Him to use His words to reveal your heart and your response to Him. If you are not sure what or how to pray, then simply read the following few verses back to God as your own prayer to Him. God promises to answer prayers that are in agreement with His will, and each of these four verses are prayers that are taken directly from His Word.

Open my eyes to see the wonderful truths in your instructions.
Psalm 119:18 (NLT)

I keep asking that the God of our Lord Jesus Christ, the glorious Father, may give you the Spirit of wisdom and revelation, so that you may know him better.
Ephesians 1:17 (NIV)

We always pray that God will show you everything he wants you to do and that you may have all the wisdom and understanding that his Spirit gives.

Colossians 1:9b (CEV)

If any of you needs wisdom to know what you should do, you should ask God, and he will give it to you. God is generous to everyone and doesn't find fault with them.

James 1:5 (GWT)

SAMPLE PRAYER:

God, I ask that You open my eyes to see the wonderful truths of Your instructions found in Your Word. I ask that You give me a Spirit of wisdom and revelation so I can know You better. I ask as I read Your Word that You would look beneath the surface, examine my life, and show me what You want me to do to become a better reflection of You. Thank You for not finding fault in my request and for giving me the desire to know Your will for my life. In Jesus name, amen.

PART I

DIRECTIONS:

Now that you have asked God to use His Word to examine your heart, the next step is to simply read the verses below and then highlight or underline any words or phrases that seem to reflect or resonate with you.

SKEPTICAL

Summary: Presented with the person of Christ and the Gospel multiple times, I demonstrate disinterest or unbelief.

Even after Jesus had done all these miraculous signs in their presence, they still would not believe in him.
John 12:37 (NIV)

Characteristics: Calloused heart, dull ears, closed eyes.

"For this people's heart has grown callous, their ears are dull of hearing, they have closed their eyes;"
Matthew 13:15a (WEB)

Christ's Next Step Invitation: Repent. Believe.

Then he began to denounce the cities in which most of his mighty works had been done, because they didn't repent.Matthew 11:20 (WEB)

Growth Barrier: A lack of spiritual understanding;

"When anyone hears the message about the kingdom and does not understand it, the evil one comes and snatches away what was sown in their heart. This is the seed sown along the path." Matthew 13:19 (NIV)

Spiritual Need: A loving and praying friend; a change of mind and heart initiated by the Holy Spirit.

He said to them, "This kind can come out by nothing, except by prayer and fasting." Mark 9:29 (WEB)

As for you, you were dead in your transgressions and sins, in which you used to live when you followed the ways of this world and of the ruler of the kingdom of the air, the spirit who is now at work in those who are disobedient
Ephesians 1:1-2 (NIV)

Seeking

Summary: Questioning, with a desire to learn more about Jesus.

He answered, "And who is he, sir? Tell me, so that I may believe in him." John 9:36 (ISV)

Characteristics: A ready heart, open ears, questions with an interest to learn more about Jesus.

Again, the next day, John was standing with two of his disciples, and he looked at Jesus as he walked, and said, "Behold, the Lamb of God!" The two disciples heard him speak, and they followed Jesus. Jesus turned, and saw them following, and said to them, "What are you looking for?" They said to him, "Rabbi" (which is to say, being interpreted, Teacher), "where are you staying?" He said to them, "Come, and see." They came and saw where he was staying, and they stayed with him that day.
John 1:35-39 (WEB)

Christ's Next Step Invitation: Repent. Believe.

Now after John was taken into custody, Jesus came into Galilee, preaching the Good News of the Kingdom of God, and saying, "The time is fulfilled, and the Kingdom of God is at hand! Repent, and believe in the Good News." Mark 1:14-15 (WEB)

Growth Barrier: A lack of clear presentation and understanding of the Gospel; a lack of invitation.

How, then, can people call on someone they have not believed? And how can they believe in someone they have not heard about? And how can they hear without someone preaching? Romans 10:14 (ISV)

Spiritual Need: A clear Gospel presentation and invitation to believe and receive salvation.

But to all who did receive him, who believed in his name, he gave the right to become children of God,
John 1:12 (ESV)

BELIEVING

Summary: Presented with the Gospel, I believe.

He said, "Lord, I believe!" and he worshiped him.
John 9:38 (WEB)

Characteristics: Seed begins to germinate, but has shallow soil and little or no roots.

Other seeds fell on rocky ground, where they did not have much soil, and immediately they sprang up, since they had no depth of soil, but when the sun rose they were scorched. And since they had no root, they withered away. Matthew 13:5-6 (ESV).

Christ's Next Step Invitation: Follow.

And he said to them, "Follow me, and I will make you fishers of men." Matthew 4:19 (ESV)

Growth Barrier: Lack of roots, lack of knowledge. Testing, trouble, persecution.

These in the same way are those who are sown on the rocky places, who, when they have heard the word, immediately receive it with joy. They have no root in themselves, but are short-lived. When oppression or persecution arises because of the word, immediately they stumble. Mark 4:16-17 (WEB)

Spiritual Need: Prayer, roots, knowledge, biblical teaching, time, worship and someone to walk with them.

Like newborn infants, long for the pure spiritual milk, that by it you may grow up into salvation.
1 Peter 2:2 (ESV)

So then, just as you received Christ Jesus as Lord, continue to live your lives in him, rooted and built up in him, strengthened in the faith as you were taught, and overflowing with thankfulness. Colossians 2:6-7 (NIV)

We continually ask God to fill you with the knowledge of his will through all the wisdom and understanding that the Spirit gives, so that you may live a life worthy of the Lord and please Him in every way: bearing fruit in every good work, growing in the knowledge of God, being strengthened with all power according to His glorious might so that you may have great endurance and patience, and giving joyful thanks to the Father, who has qualified you to share in the inheritance of His holy people in the kingdom of light. Colossians 1:9-12 (NIV)

FOLLOWING

Summary: Growing in faith and love, deepening roots and knowledge, struggling with thorns, trials, forgiveness, doubt, and perseverance.

By this all people will know that you are my disciples, if you have love for one another." John 13:35 (ESV)

Characteristics: Beginning to push through the soil, struggling with thorns and weeds.

Other seeds fell among thorns, and the thorns grew up and choked them. Matthew 13:7 (WEB)

And calling the crowd to him with his disciples, he said to them, "If anyone would come after me, let him deny himself and take up his cross and follow me."
Mark 8:34 (ESV)

Christ's Next Step Invitation: Deny self, pick up cross, trust, obey, and love Christ and others.

Then Jesus said to his disciples, "If anyone desires to come after me, let him deny himself, and take up his cross, and follow me."
Matthew 16:24 (WEB)

Growth Barrier: Thorns, worries of this life, doubt, deceitfulness of wealth, comfort, self and self will.

Others are those who are sown among the thorns. These are those who have heard the word, and the cares of this age, and the deceitfulness of riches, and the lusts of other things entering in choke the word, and it becomes unfruitful. Mark 4:18-19 (WEB)

Spiritual Need: Deny self, trials, endurance, perseverance, time, small group relationships and accountability.

Consider it pure joy, my brothers and sisters whenever you face trials of many kinds, because you know that the testing of your faith produces perseverance.

Let perseverance finish its work so that you may be mature and complete, not lacking anything.
James 1:2-4 (NIV)

Through him we have also obtained access by faith into this grace in which we stand, and we rejoice in hope of the glory of God. More than that, we rejoice in our sufferings, knowing that suffering produces endurance, and endurance produces character, and character produces hope, Romans 5:2-4 (ESV)

These have come so that the proven genuineness of your faith—of greater worth than gold, which perishes even though refined by fire may result in praise, glory and honor when Jesus Christ is revealed.
1 Peter 1:7 (NIV)

FRIEND

Marked by obedient love for Christ and :estle with isolation, complacency, and

red.

"You are my friends if you do what I command you."
John 15:14 (ESV)

Characteristics: Good soil, obedience to Christ, fruit, growing faith, increasing love and perseverance in trials.

Your faith is growing more and more, and the love all of you have for one another is increasing. Therefore, among God's churches we boast about your perseverance and faith in all the persecutions and trials you are enduring.
2 Thessalonians 1:3-4 (NIV)

Christ's Next Step Invitation: Love, obey, go, teach.

"If you love me, you will keep my commandments"
John 14:15 (ESV)

"You are my friends if you do what I command you."
John 15:14 (ESV)

Jesus came to them and spoke to them, saying, "All authority has been given to me in heaven and on earth. Therefore go, and make disciples of all nations, baptizing them in the name of the Father and of the Son and of the Holy Spirit, teaching them to observe all things that I commanded you. Behold, I am with you always, even to the end of the age." Amen. Matthew 28:18-20 (WEB)

Growth Barrier: Complacency, fear, pride, lack of vision and lack of equipping.

Then he said to his disciples, "The harvest indeed is plentiful, but the laborers are few."
Matthew 9:37 (WEB)

How, then, can people call on someone they have not
believed? And how can they believe in someone they
have not heard about? And how can they hear without
someone preaching? Romans 10:14 (ISV)

Spiritual Need: Vision, continued obedience, equipping,
empowerment, continued spurring and accountability
within community.

To prepare God's people for works of service, so that the
body of Christ may be built up until we all reach unity in
the faith and in the knowledge of the Son of God and
become mature, attaining to the whole measure of the
fullness of Christ. Ephesians 4:12-13 (NIV)

As for you, brothers, do not grow weary in doing good.
                              2 Thessalonians 3:13 (ESV)

Let us continue to hold firmly to the hope that we
confess without wavering, for the one who made the
promise is faithful. And let us continue to consider how
to motivate one another to love and good deeds, not
neglecting to meet together, as is the habit of some, but
encouraging one another even more as you see the day of
the Lord coming nearer. Hebrews 10:23-25 (ISV)

FISHERMAN

Summary: Reflecting Christ and reproducing fruit of
righteousness and good works.

Because we have heard of your faith in Christ Jesus and
of the love you have for all God's people—the faith and
love that spring from the hope stored up for you in
heaven and about which you have already heard in the
true message of the gospel that has come to you. In the

same way, the gospel is bearing fruit and growing throughout the whole world—just as it has been doing among you since the day you heard it and truly understood God's grace Colossians 1:5-6 (NIV)

Characteristics: Good soil, fruitfulness, harvest, influence, reflecting Christ.

Others fell on good soil, and yielded fruit: some one hundred times as much, some sixty, and some thirty.
Matthew 13:8 (WEB)

Christ's Next Step Invitation: Teach others.

Therefore, as you go, disciple people in all nations, baptizing them in the name of the Father, and the Son, and the Holy Spirit, teaching them to obey everything that I've commanded you." Matthew 28:19-20a (ISV)

Growth Barrier: Complacency, fear, pride, lack of vision, lack of equipping and weariness.

Let's not get tired of doing what is good, for at the right time we will reap a harvest-if we do not give up.
Galatians 6:9 (ISV)

Think about the one who endured such hostility from sinners, so that you may not become tired and give up.
Hebrews 12:3 (ISV)

Spiritual Need: Perseverance, humility, faithfulness, accountability with reliable people.

It gave me great joy when some believers came and testified about your faithfulness to the truth, telling how you continue to walk in it. 3 John 1:3 (NIV)

And what you have heard from me in the presence of many witnesses entrust to faithful men who will be able to teach others also. 2 Timothy 2:2 (ESV)

100. Christ-centered.

PART II

Directions: Consider the words or phrases you highlighted or underlined and answer the following seven questions.

1. WHERE AM I?

Skeptic: When presented with the Gospel, I do not believe.

Seeker: Questioning, with a desire to learn more about Jesus.

Believer: Presented with the Gospel, I chose to believe.

Follower: Growing in faith, love, and roots, struggling with thorns, trials and perseverance.

Friend: Marked by obedient love for Christ and others.

Fisherman: Reflecting Christ and bearing fruit of righteousness and good works.

2. WHERE WOULD I LIKE TO BE IN SIX MONTHS?

Skeptic: When presented with the Gospel, I do not to believe.

Seeker: Questioning, with a desire to learn more about Jesus.

Believer: Presented with the Gospel, I chose to believe.

Follower: Growing in faith, love, and roots, struggling with thorns, trials and perseverance.

Friend: Marked by obedient love for Christ and others.

Fisherman: Reflecting Christ and bearing fruit of righteousness and good works.

3. WHAT INVITATION DO I NEED TO RESPOND TO IN ORDER TO TAKE MY NEXT STEP?

Skeptic: Repent.

Seeker: Repent. Believe.

Believer: Follow.

Follower: Deny self. Pick up cross. Obey. Love Christ and others.

Friend: Love. Obey. Go.

Fisherman: Teach others.

4. WHAT BARRIERS WILL I FACE?

Skeptic: Calloused heart, deaf ears, closed eyes.

Seeker: Lack of clear testimony. Lack of invitation.

Believer: Lack of roots. Testing, trouble, persecution.

Follower: Thorns. Worries of this life. Deceitfulness of wealth. Comfort. Self.

Friend: Complacency. Fear. Lack of vision. Lack of equipping.

Fisherman: Complacency. Fear. Lack of vision. Lack of equipping. Weariness.

5. WHAT SPIRITUAL NEEDS DO I HAVE?

Skeptic: Prayer. Repentance. Believing friends.

Seeker: Receive. Believe. Salvation.

Believer: Prayer. Roots. Knowledge. Teaching. Worship. Time.

Follower: Deny self. Trials. Endurance. Perseverance. Time. Small group relationships and accountability.

Friend: Vision. Continued obedience. Equipping. Opportunity. Empowerment and accountability within community.

Fisherman: Perseverance. Faithfulness. Reliable people.

6. WHAT STEPS WILL I TAKE?

7. WHO WILL I ASK TO HOLD ME ACCOUNTABLE?

Part III

Next Steps

Now that you have answered the seven questions and outlined a plan, do not wait to begin taking your next steps. Contact the person you identified to hold you accountable and share with them what God showed you through the reflection process. If you have a small group, share the assessment with them and then offer to encourage one another as you take your next steps toward becoming reflections of Christ.

Here are some verses to encourage you as you move forward.

> But don't just listen to God's word. You must do what it says. Otherwise, you are only fooling yourselves.
>
> James 1:22 (NLT)

> And we also thank God continually because, when you received the word of God, which you heard from us, you accepted it not as the word of men, but as it actually is, the word of God, which is at work in you who believe.
>
> 1 Thessalonians 2:13 (NIV)

> Perseverance must finish its work so that you may be mature and complete, not lacking anything.
>
> James 1:4 (NIV)

I'm convinced that God, who began this good work in you, will carry it through to completion on the day of Christ Jesus.

Philippians 1:6 (GWT)

For God is working in you, giving you the desire and the power to do what pleases him.

Philippians 2:13 (NLT)

So, then, brothers and sisters, don't let anyone move you off the foundation [of your faith]. Always excel in the work you do for the Lord. You know that the hard work you do for the Lord is not pointless.

1 Corinthians 15:58 (GWT)

But encourage one another day after day, as long as it is still called "Today," so that none of you will be hardened by the deceitfulness of sin.

Hebrews 13:3 (NASB)

Reflection

1. What ideas or images stood out to you in this book?

2. What was refreshing? Why?

3. What was frustrating? Why?

4. What questions do you have?

CHAPTER 6

EMPOWERED BY LOVE

I hated taking tests in school. For whatever reason, it always seemed like I never studied the right material, and I struggled with the problem of second-guessing my answers. I could literally talk myself in or out of just about any answer on any exam.

It was not until I became a teacher that I found out the purpose of evaluations. The intent of an assessment is not to fool you or trick you. It's not to make you feel foolish or bad about yourself. The purpose of a good examination is to discover where you are in the learning process in order for the teacher to help you learn. It is to help the teacher identify what learning gaps you may have and how to adjust the curriculum to meet your learning needs. Learning is not about the assessments. Assessments are simply a tool to help you learn.

The same is true about spiritual growth. Spiritual growth is not about the assessment. The evaluation is only helpful if it equips us with the right information. By itself, an examination can never be transformational; it can only be informational. Consider this truth: The Gospels record people having conversations with Jesus. Some people respond to Jesus well. Some don't. Jesus is the living, breathing, Word of God. Jesus, the Word of God, uses His words and His invitations to assess the hearts of people in order to teach to their spiritual needs and to any obstacles to spiritual growth. That is how He moved people through the process of spiritual growth, by assessing or examining the soil of their heart through how they responded to His words.

At this point in the book, it may still feel a bit like a large puzzle that has not yet been put together. All of the pieces are there, but things may not be clear yet. The value of the parable of the sower becomes clearer in light of Christ's explanation.

FROM INFORMED TO TRANSFORMED

Some people responded with skeptical, callous hearts. Others responded with hearts that desired to know more about Him, but their hearts lacked spiritual roots and needed to learn His yoke. Still others, the disciples, were aware of His teaching, but they needed to move it from their heads to their hearts through the process of not just knowing about God, but trusting Him over themselves and loving Him while denying

108. Christ-centered.

themselves. Finally, there were those who heard the word of God, responded with loving obedience, and bore fruit in their lives that they needed to go and teach others about.

> How you and I hear and respond to the word of God reveals our hearts toward God and helps us identify what stage of growth we are in, but Christ moves us from one stage of growth to the next.

Assessments need to do more than give facts; they should lead us toward results. For example, it is not enough to simply step on a scale to realize how over or under weight we might be or to receive the results of a blood test that inform us of problems with our cholesterol without taking action in response to that information. Without an action plan we are simply informed. Not transformed.

PROFILES OF OUR HEARTS

In the same way, if you are not sure where you are in the growth process of reflecting Christ and you do not have a plan for the next step based on your specific spiritual need or spiritual obstacle, then your assessment is an effort in futility.

What is cool about following Jesus is that He acts as a personal trainer for each of us. His goal is to invite us into His personal process of transformation and not simply to invite us to a series of dry classes. He desires for the Word of God to be used to equip us with understanding so that we can respond in a way that will bear fruit in our lives.

As we learned in Isaiah 28, God gives wisdom to farmers so that they do not do the same thing over and over or treat every plant and every season the same. Each season demands different types of treatment, and each plant invites individual attention.

Jesus gives us the same insight and wisdom into our spiritual needs and obstacles. In the parable of the soil, He profiles each heart. Some hearts are hard and unreceptive to the Word of God. We see religious leaders and other skeptics respond to Jesus in this manner. We see Christ give invitations to people who respond to the word of by turning and walking away. Jesus never chases after them. Why? Because the Holy Spirit has not prepared their hearts to hear and respond to the Word of God, and Jesus does not want to callous their hearts. Instead He instructs us that hard hearts can only be changed through prayer and the power of the Spirit.

There are some people who respond readily to the Word of God with great joy. These new believers are hungry, but they lack roots that will allow them to last. You and I have seen what this looks like, perhaps in our own lives when we have an exciting, emotional experience in our relationship with Christ only to find our feelings fizzle a few weeks or months later. Jesus tells us people at this stage of growth must be filled with knowledge and truth in order to sustain the difficulties of life.[1] It is like the trees in my yard that must have deep

110. Christ-centered.

roots to endure and survive the hot summer months and seasons of drought.

The apostle Paul builds on Jesus' profile by telling the church in Ephesus they need to be rooted and established.[2] Jesus addresses the needs of these new believers by giving some of His longest sermons and, in so doing, presenting people with His yoke. At that point, He did not expect them to remember everything, but He recognized their need for deep roots, for the ability to understand what it looks like to follow Him and what they should expect in the process.

Christ also recognized that His goal was not to make large crowds of students who had head knowledge about Him, but who failed to become disciple-making disciples, so He sent out the seventy two disciples[3] in order for them to put into practice what He had been teaching them.

Christ also knew that these informed disciples had to be tested in order to identify the weeds that still gripped their hearts and could potentially cripple their growth. He informed them that they will face trials and struggles, not because He has forsaken them, but because they must learn to trust Him. In order for those at that stage to take their next step and to truly reach maturity, they must learn that He is trustworthy and dependable. This can only be learned through the trials, testing, and refining of their faith. Christ's path for the disciples helps us make sense of life. It tells us what to expect and gives some answers as to why trials are not only a natural part of our spiritual growth, but a needed part.

Now when trials and testing come, we can respond with understanding rather than shock and disappointment. Without understanding Christ's process of moving our hearts from self-centeredness and self-dependency to Christ-centeredness and Christ-dependency, we are left to our own ideas of how and why things are happening the way they do. We are left to think that perhaps God forgot us or abandoned us, when in reality His love leads us into maturity. We believe the devil's lies that perhaps He is punishing us when the truth of God's word and His plan proclaim that it is His love that leads Him to discipline and disciple us.

A HARVEST OF RIGHTEOUSNESS

Understanding bears fruit. Understanding gives us the clarity and confidence to continue to repent and change our minds and understanding about Jesus and who He is and how He is at work in our lives. Understanding continues to deepen our beliefs so that our faith in Him and His process is firmly rooted and established. Understanding allows us to enter into trials and temptations prepared to trust the God who invites us to love Him and deny ourselves without the baggage of lies from our enemies. Understanding bears the fruit that allows us to respond to the invitation to go and teach others with the understanding that we ourselves have received. Do not take my word for it. Examine for

112. Christ-centered.

yourself to see what the Word of God says:

> And have you completely forgotten this word of
> encouragement that addresses you as a father
> addresses his son? It says,

> "My son, do not make light of the Lord's discipline,
> and do not lose heart when he rebukes you, because
> the Lord disciplines the one he loves and he chastens
> everyone he accepts as his son."

> Endure hardship as discipline; God is treating you as
> his children. For what children are not disciplined by
> their father?
>
> Hebrews 12:5-7 (NIV)

> If you are not disciplined—and everyone undergoes
> discipline—then you are not legitimate, not true sons
> and daughters at all. Moreover, we have all had
> human fathers who disciplined us and we respected
> them for it. How much more should we submit to
> the Father of spirits and live! They disciplined us for
> a little while as they thought best; but God
> disciplines us for our good, in order that we may
> share in his holiness.

> No discipline seems pleasant at the time, but painful.
> Later on, however, it produces a harvest of
> righteousness and peace for those who have been
> trained by it.
>
> Hebrews 12:8-11 (NIV)

But the seed falling on good soil refers to someone who hears the word and understands it. This is the one who produces a crop, yielding a hundred, sixty or thirty times what was sown."

Matthew 13:23 NIV)

Let us then approach God's throne of grace with confidence, so that we may receive mercy and find grace to help us in our time of need.

Hebrews 4:16 (NIV)

For this reason I kneel before the Father, from whom every family in heaven and on earth derives its name. I pray that out of his glorious riches he may strengthen you with power through his Spirit in your inner being, so that Christ may dwell in your hearts through faith.

And I pray that you, being rooted and established in love, may have power, together with all the Lord's holy people, to grasp how wide and long and high and deep is the love of Christ, and to know this love that surpasses knowledge—that you may be filled to the measure of all the fullness of God.

Ephesians 3:14-19 (NIV)

Consider it pure joy, my brothers and sisters, whenever you face trials of many kinds, because you know that the testing of your faith produces perseverance. Let perseverance finish its work so that you may be mature and complete, not lacking anything.

James 1:2-4 (NIV)

What then shall we say, brothers and sisters? When you come together, each of you has a hymn, or a word of instruction, a revelation, a tongue or an interpretation. Everything must be done so that the church may be built up.

1 Corinthians 14:26 (NIV)

Preach the word; be prepared in season and out of season; correct, rebuke and encourage—with great patience and careful instruction.

2 Timothy 4:2 (NIV)

As we continue to grow in our understanding of Christ and His process of making disciples, we can spend less time attempting to create our own plans and more time learning how to respond to His plan and how to carefully instruct others.

RECOGNIZING OUR DEPENDENCE

As we learn to respond to His invitations and participate in His plan, we can stop the religious activities of doing things for Christ and begin reacting to what He has already done for us. In other words, we can stop reading the Bible and attending church in order to check religious activities off of a list, and we can begin learning how to read and understand the word of God in a way that will allow us to apply it to our lives accurately.

The important thing to understand is that God has chosen to reveal His supernatural process for transforming our will into a reflection of His. It is not through religious activities or even spiritual disciplines; it is through learning to identify and respond to His invitations with understanding. It is the epitome of relationship. Jesus invites us to be with Him through the Word of God so that He can reveal Himself to us and induce us to take on His attributes. What makes it difficult is that it is the opposite of religion that is based on rules and lists.

We tend to love rules because we can understand rules. Just tell me what to do and I'll do it. We gravitate toward things that we can control, and rules give us a false sense of control. Relationships are messy. Even when we understand how Christ works and accept His invitation to study these passages further, our temptation is to remove the supernatural element from it and to codify Christ's process of inviting us to respond to Him with the creation of another program. Once we understand how something works, our natural tendency is to remove the supernatural mystery by relying on our own understanding and remove the supernatural element from it.

But just because we understand how something works does not make something any less of an act of God. Just because we understand how the weather works does not mean that God is no longer in control; or just because we understand how a baby develops in the womb does not make it cease to be an entirely supernatural and miraculous occurrence. No, in reality the fact that God has allowed us the glimpse of Himself through the patterns of the weather or through the miracle of birth makes it all the more a reflection of His supernatural power.

> In the same way, just because we understand how Christ's process of moving people from self-centered, self-sufficient lives to a life centered on Christ and His sufficiency does not make it any less miraculous. Understanding simply makes room for the Spirit of God to work in our lives and to bear fruit.

We are not less dependent upon God and His Spirit because He answers our prayer to give us understanding; we can now rest in our dependency with the certainty that comes from understanding.

WISDOM FROM GOD

God gives wisdom that allows us to understand our role in the process of growth. God is still the one who changes hearts. He invites us to follow Him with the wisdom He gives rather than the ignorance of our collective thoughts and programs. He shows us His methods so that we can do our part of sowing the seeds of His word with the confidence that comes from understanding that He will be faithful to do His part and illuminate hearts.

His wisdom invites us to approach His word to examine our hearts with understanding in the same way He invited His disciples to learn how to respond to Him.

Our confidence comes not from ourselves, but in the increased understanding of our dependence on the reality of God at work in and through our lives.

We do not manipulate God to do our bidding. We learn to hear His voice through the understanding that He gives of the promise of His Word and the power of His Spirit. It is with anticipation of His promise to make us into His reflections that we rest in His hands as He mold our hearts to accurately reflect His own heart and will.

Consider some of what Scripture has to say about this process of growing in our understanding. God invites us and makes promises throughout Scripture to guide His people through wisdom and understanding that He gives:

> …Turning your ear to wisdom
> and applying your heart to understanding
> > Proverbs 2:2 (NIV)

> For the Lord gives wisdom; from his mouth come knowledge and understanding.
> > Proverbs 2:6 (NIV)

> Trust in the Lord with all your heart
> and lean not on your own understanding;
> in all your ways submit to him,
> and he will make your paths straight.
> > Proverbs 3:5-6 (NIV)

Then I will give you shepherds after my own heart, who will lead you with knowledge and understanding.

Jeremiah 3:15 (NIV)

Then he continued, "Do not be afraid, Daniel. Since the first day that you set your mind to gain understanding and to humble yourself before your God, your words were heard, and I have come in response to them.

Daniel 10:12 (NIV)

For this reason, since the day we heard about you, we have not stopped praying for you. We continually ask God to fill you with the knowledge of his will through all the wisdom and understanding that the Spirit gives.

Colossians 1:9 (NIV)

We know also that the Son of God has come and has given us understanding, so that we may know him who is true.

1 John 5:20a (NIV)

He gives us insight and wisdom, not so that we may grow in our self-confidence, but in Christ-centered reverence and reflection:

And we all, who with unveiled faces contemplate the Lord's glory, are being transformed into his image with ever-increasing glory, which comes from the Lord, who is the Spirit.

2 Corinthians 3:18 (NIV)

Therefore, since we have these promises, dear friends, let us purify ourselves from everything that contaminates body and spirit, perfecting holiness out of reverence for God.

2 Corinthians 7:1 (NIV)

You became imitators of us and of the Lord, for you welcomed the message in the midst of severe suffering with the joy given by the Holy Spirit.

1 Thessalonians 1:6 (NIV)

Again and again, Paul warns and reminds believers that our understanding should increase our dependence, not our independence:

I would like to learn just one thing from you: Did you receive the Spirit by the works of the law, or by believing what you heard?

Galatians 3:2 (NIV)

Are you so foolish? After beginning by means of the Spirit, are you now trying to finish by means of the flesh?

Galatians 3:3 (NIV)

So how will we respond to this gracious gift of understanding and invitation to apply Christ's wisdom to our lives? We should take note from the words of James, brother of Jesus, that we need to do more than simply become aware of this insight; we need to apply it to our lives.

Do not merely listen to the word, and so deceive yourselves. Do what it says. Anyone who listens to the word but does not do what it says is like someone who looks at his face in a mirror and, after looking at himself, goes away and immediately forgets what he looks like.

But whoever looks intently into the perfect law that gives freedom, and continues in it—not forgetting what they have heard, but doing it—they will be blessed in what they do.

James 1:22-25 (NIV)

How do we keep from just becoming hearers and failing to become doers of His word?

Too often a message is falsely communicated that we need to respond to the Lord out of gratitude for what He has done and accomplished for us. He died for you, so out of gratitude we should live for Him. But the truth is that gratitude is not enough. Gratitude is something that can be self-manufactured. Christ's actions and invitations have sovereign rights to our responses, but it is only through His Spirit that we can experience true empowerment. That is why Jesus said, "Apart from me you can do nothing[4]." Included in the word "nothing" is everything, and included in everything is our ability and motivation to respond to Him.

Our motivation to respond to Christ is entirely dependent upon Him. It is not something that we can self-manufacture or self-sustain.

EMPOWERED TO RESPOND

In John 14:15, Jesus taught that those who love Him will obey Him and they will be the ones that He calls His friends. In saying this, Jesus recognizes the difference between causes and outcomes.

Too often we are focused on the outcomes of spiritual growth. Are we doing the right things? Are we being obedient? But as a parent, I can tell you that there are times when my kids obey me on the outside and yet their hearts are sometimes far from me.

Jesus is always more concerned about how our hearts are responding to him than whether or not we are performing the right actions. He is always more concerned about the cause than the outcome.

For example, in 1 Samuel 13:1-15, King Saul performed the sacrifice of worship, but his motivation was fear and his act of disobedience resulted in grave consequence for him and those who followed him.

Jesus does not want the redemption of our actions; He desires the redemption of our hearts. There are plenty of people performing miraculous acts of kindness for their own glory and pleasure; there are plenty of people who pray and perform religious activities hoping to earn the favor of God or men, but God desires that our motivation is our love for Him. The only way we will grow in love for Him is when we learn to trust Him through trials over time.

That is why Paul wrote to the young pastor of the church in Ephesus that he should not choose leaders who had the right answers, but ones who had been tested and who had proven that they had pure hearts.[5]

Just because we have a basic level of understanding of what to expect does not make the process of spiritual transformation easier.

Even under the power of the Holy Spirit, transformation is difficult because we experience the death of our pride, self-sufficiency, and desires as they are being replaced with humility, dependency, and the will of God for our lives.

> In your relationships with one another,
>   have the same mindset as Christ Jesus:
>
> Who, being in very nature God,
>   did not consider equality with God something to
> be used to his own advantage;
>
> rather, he made himself nothing
>   by taking the very nature of a servant,
>   being made in human likeness.
>
> And being found in appearance as a man,
>   he humbled himself
>   by becoming obedient to death—
> even death on a cross!
>
>   Philippians 2:6-8 (NIV)

DISCIPLINE YOURSELVES

In order to have the mindset of Christ, we must continually work to hear His voice as we learn to respond to His invitations. But His enemy and ours will continually attempt to drown out the voice of our shepherd through other noises and voices in this world.

> But in the midst of the noise Christ will keep whispering that He is sufficient and desires to be with us and for us to follow Him.

That is where spiritual disciplines come in. Spiritual disciplines are not about doing something for Jesus; they are about learning to silence the other voices and noises of the world so that we can tune in to hear the voice of Christ.

> Without prayer, fasting is simply starvation. Without the truth of God's word, meditation is simply babbling empty-headedness.

> And when you pray, do not keep on babbling like pagans, for they think they will be heard because of their many words.
>
> Matthew 6:7 (NIV)

The purpose of solitude is to train ourselves to distinguish His voice. The purpose of studying the Word of God is to fix our eyes on Jesus, because when we take our eyes off Jesus and place them on our trials, we will be tempted to question the truths of His abilities and sink back into old habits.

This was the experience of Peter walking on the water. When his eyes were fixed on His Savior, he experienced the transforming confidence and the fruit of God's spirit of peace that passes all understanding. In contrast, when he looked at the waves, he began to sink into his fears.

LEARNING TO LOVE

Jesus knows that in order to follow Him in obedience, we must learn to love Him. In order to love Him, we must learn to trust Him through trials and temptations over time. It is only through this process that our hearts will be motivated by love to proclaim our full dependency. In the words of John the Baptizer we will say:

> "He must increase while I must decrease."
>
> John 3:30 (ESV)

Later, when Paul would say, "Not I, but Christ,"[6] he is echoing the words of John the Baptizer who said, "He must increase, but I must decrease."[7]

> I have been crucified with Christ and I no longer live, but Christ lives in me. The life I now live in the body, I live by faith in the Son of God, who loved me and gave himself for me.
>
> Galatians 2:20 (NIV)

Consider these words from an aging Apostle Paul reflecting back upon his journey with Christ toward maturity:

> But whatever were gains to me I now consider loss for the sake of Christ. What is more, I consider everything a loss because of the surpassing worth of knowing Christ Jesus my Lord, for whose sake I have lost all things. I consider them garbage, that I may gain Christ and be found in him, not having a righteousness of my own that comes from the law, but that which is through faith in Christ—the righteousness that comes from God on the basis of faith. I want to know Christ—yes, to know the power of his resurrection and participation in his sufferings, becoming like him in his death, and so, somehow, attaining to the resurrection from the dead.
>
> Philippians 3:7-11

WHAT DO YOU LOVE?

By the end of John's and Paul's lives, they had learned to trust God through trials of many kinds, but instead of growing bitter or speaking of an increase in self-sufficiency, they both spoke of an increased desire to know Christ and be found in Him.

What motivates you as you face the future? Is it an increased love for your Savior and Rabbi? Or are you still operating out of a sense of self-sufficiency that depends on your own strength to achieve your own goals?

As you face the next steps in your process of transformation you too will face trials of many kinds. How will you respond?

CHAPTER 7

THE PROMISE
OF CHRIST

STAYING CHRIST-CENTERED

Christ's invitations are a simple process. The night I stood in front of a large whiteboard and realized how all of the pieces fit together was pretty amazing. I had to read, search, and empty myself of my own ideas in order to accept more of Christ's.

In retrospect, I believe the journey God took me through to discover His process was more important to Him than my desire to acquire answers. During that prolonged season of searching, there was a verse that I clung to as both equally challenging and comforting.

> It is the glory of God to conceal a matter; to search out a matter is the glory of kings.
>
> Proverbs 25:2 (NIV)

There were times during the long nights and weekends when I was buried in references and cross-references that felt like a treasure hunt. There were other times of pure frustration and multiple dead ends.

But over the past several years as I've taught these principles in seminars around the world and watched people uncover Christ's invitations for themselves, it never ceases to give me goose bumps to recognize the same Holy Spirit illuminates the same Word of God to all of us.

Unfortunately, the average Christian has acquired the belief that spiritual growth happens when we learn to depend upon Christ for the things we cannot do on our own. But it is just the opposite that is true. What is more difficult to grasp is that spiritual growth occurs through learning to depend on Him for the things we think we can do on our own. Because apart from Him we can do nothing.[1]

His invitations are designed to lead us into deeper dependence not independence.

Apart from Christ, patience is merely a characteristic of personality and not a fruit of the spirit. There are gifts of God's grace, such as the sun and the rain, that are common to those who follow as well as those who do not.

> He causes his sun to rise on the evil and the good,
> and sends rain on the righteous and the unrighteous.
> Matthew 5:45 (NIV)

After years of growing in recognition of my total dependence upon Christ for uncovering His process of growth, as I stood looking at the simplicity of Jesus' invitations in front of me on the whiteboard, I was deluded into thinking that now things would get easier.

They didn't.

Now that spiritual growth makes sense, don't think that it will get easier. It will just become more understandable. Do not believe that it will become less difficult; it won't. It just becomes easier to identify what God desires to do in our lives, but this does not imply independence from our need for His power in the process.

Too often we look at what Christ did and miss the truths of how He related to the Father and depended upon the Spirit in His own journey. Christ's invitation to follow and to imitate Him is impossible apart from understanding and embracing the full humanity of Christ through the incarnation.

Without Christ at the center of our discipleship, we risk participating in religious activity that will keep us busy but leave us powerless. Listen to this warning Paul regarding how important it is to recognize the supremacy of Christ and how easy it is to lose focus:

You received Christ Jesus as Lord. So keep on living in him. Have your roots in him. Build yourselves up in him. Grow strong in what you believe, just as you were taught. Be more thankful than ever before. Make sure no one captures you. They will try to capture you by using false reasoning that has no meaning. Their ideas depend on human teachings. They also depend on the basic things the people of this world believe. They don't depend on Christ.

God's whole nature is living in Christ in human form. Because you belong to Christ, you have everything you need. He is the ruler over every power and authority.

Colossians 2:6-10 (NIRV)

Paul's words are as penetrating as they are stinging. Do we really believe that in Christ we have everything we need? Do we lose focus on Him due in part (or in whole) to a belief that He is not capable or sufficient in and of Himself? We must never forget at the core of Christ's invitations is His promise to transform us, but it is difficult to experience change when we lose focus and return to our own wills and our own programs. We must be careful to heed Paul's admonition to the church in Galatia when he wrote:

Are you so foolish? After beginning by means of the Spirit, are you now trying to finish by means of the flesh?

Galatians 3:3 (NIV)

To reflect Christ, we must follow Christ.

The word "incarnation" means, "God with flesh on." Tucked in the middle of the word incarnation is the root *carne* which means, "meat." Understood literally, *incarnation* means, "God with meat on." Jesus is God with flesh on, and He perfectly reflects the Father in absolute dependence upon the Holy Spirit in order that we might have the right perspective of what it means to imitate or reflect the Father.

Jesus could have chosen to come during any time in history and use any method to give the information we need to learn to reflect Him. He chose to be a rabbi. This means that even Christ's relationship with the Father and dependence upon the Spirit were part of His example for us.

Rabbis invested in disciples who would become imitations of the rabbi and who would reflect and reproduce the rabbis life and teaching. To uncover Christ's rabbinical model, we begin by returning to His rabbinical invitation:

Follow me and I will make you fishers of men.
Matthew 4:19 (ESV)

Within the first two words of Christ's primary invitation to become His disciples, "Follow Me," we are not only reminded that Christ is the one who initiates the invitation but that He is the one who must remain the center of our focus. He is the one we are to follow in every way. If anyone or anything other than Christ is at the center of our discipleship, then it is not truly Christ who we are following.

Other things subtly creep and crowd our concentration on Christ alone. In order to assess if we are actually staying centered on Christ and not getting off track, we regularly examine our motivations and goals. Paul writes it like this:

> We demolish arguments and every pretension that sets itself up against the knowledge of God, and we take captive every thought to make it obedient to Christ.
>
> 2 Corinthians 10:5 (NIV)

- Is our goal for responding to an invitation of Christ to become a better person?
- Is our goal to enjoy a better life?
- Is our goal to get rid of a bad habit, or to remove the consequences of a bad habit?
- Are we trying to earn the favor of God, or are we falsely attempting a transactional relationship with God?
- Do we treat God as a genie in a bottle who must obey if we act or speak in the right way?

These lead us back to self-centered dependency that expects God to obey and serve us.

Our goal in following Christ is not to become a missionary, or to earn God's favor, or to increase our salvation, or to become a better person or enjoy a nicer life. Those pursuits are self-centered, not Christ-centered. Pride in our own effort and desire to become better people leads us back into the world of religion that depends upon works for our salvation or subsequent maturity rather than on Christ and the power of His Holy Spirit.

When we find the transformed disciples in the book of Acts, they are each recognized as men who had been with Jesus. The more we are with Jesus, the more we will understand the depths of His love for us, and our hearts will become further bent toward Him in such a way as to reflect Him as the object of our focus and love.

Christ-centered discipleship means that our eyes are fixed on Jesus. We go where He leads under the power of His Spirit. Period. No questions asked. But that does not mean that we check our brains at the door and seek a mystical experience. We are commanded to love the Lord our God with all of our minds and to participate in a reasoned and reasonable faith.[2] This means that we need to become students of Christ and His words, because we can only learn to become like Christ when we intentionally choose to be with Christ and allow Him to renew our minds:

> Therefore, I urge you, brothers and sisters, in view of God's mercy, to offer your bodies as a living sacrifice, holy and pleasing to God—this is your true and proper worship. Do not conform to the pattern

of this world, but be transformed by the renewing of your mind. Then you will be able to test and approve what God's will is—his good, pleasing and perfect will.

Romans 12:1-2 (NIV)

Renewed minds begin when we respond to His invitation. He changes our minds and replaces our false assumptions and conceptions with the reality of His truth. To follow Christ means we need to hear His voice, but in order to follow Him, we must also learn to trust Him:

> My sheep hear My voice, and I know them, and they follow Me.
>
> John 10:27 (NASB)

Our goal is to be with Jesus. When we learn to identify His voice and respond to His invitations, He transforms us into His reflections. Following Christ and listening to His voice demands that we have both the courage and humility to submit to His leadership. This means we need to check our frustration at the door when His direction does not match our thoughts and desires. We must trust that His directions have our best interests in mind even when we do not understand them. This level of trust takes time. Jesus not only knows this, but He understands and invites us to take His yoke and learn to trust ourselves to Him.

> Take my yoke upon you and learn from Me, for I am gentle and humble in heart, and you will find rest for your souls. Matthew 11:29 (NASB)

BUT THIS TAKES TIME.

It takes approximately 10,000 hours of deliberate and intentional practice to become an expert at something. This theory was explained in a 1993 paper by Dr. Anders Ericsson and popularized in the book *Outliers*, by Malcolm Gladwell. To put those numbers in perspective, the average person who puts in twenty hours per week for fifty weeks per year for ten years can acquire a mastery of whatever they have intentionally and deliberately practiced. Both Gladwell and Ericsson are quick to point out that these 10,000 hours are hours dedicated to intentional and deliberate practice.

To support the theory, Gladwell uncovers the histories of several "overnight successes" to reveal the truth that behind the scenes it was not dumb luck or natural skill, but a long process of quietly acquiring 10,000 hours of deliberate, intentional practice to become experts in their particular field.

Keep that in mind and consider our scenario with Christ and His disciples. They had both macro and micro motivation to initially drop their nets and follow Him, but learning to trust Him took time. Consider that even at the end of two and a half years together they all still struggled to believe He was actually resurrected from the dead. Jesus knew this would be the case. They would not be able to trust, reflect, and reproduce Christ overnight. That is why He invested time being with them.

He appointed twelve that they might be with him
and that he might send them out to preach.
Mark 3:14 (NIV)

Have you ever stopped to figure out exactly how
many hours Christ invested in being with His disciples?
Would you be surprised to learn that it was about 10,000
hours?

We can figure out from the Gospel record that between
the time when Christ called His disciples and the time He
ascended into heaven was approximately two and a half
years. When we consider the daily relationship between a
disciple and their rabbi to be an average of twelve hours a
day (taking into account times for sleeping or other
activities) and multiple that by one hundred thirty weeks,
the result is 10,920 hours.

Modern science tells us that in order to move an
average person with no skill from entry level to mastery is
10,000 hours of deliberate and intentional practice. Jesus
models for us a process of discipleship in which His
disciples followed Him deliberately and intentionally for
roughly 10,000 hours

So let me ask you: Where are your 10,000 hours
going? Based on the current amount of time you are
investing in deliberate time directly with Jesus, how long
before you reach 10,000 hours? Remember, these hours
only include the time you are deliberately and
intentionally focused on your relationship with Christ, not
the hours where you are daydreaming through a sermon.

Let's do some math together. 10,000 hours consists of 600,000 minutes. Let's assume we invest thirty minutes a day, five days a week in focused study of God's word.. Perhaps you have a larger number, or perhaps your number is smaller, but let's start with thirty minutes and see where we end up.

Thirty minutes a day of deliberate and intentional focus on Christ become 10,950 minutes a year; and at 10,950 minutes a year you would reach 600,000 minutes in approximately fifty five years from whenever you started. Perhaps thirty minutes a day isn't your number. Perhaps it is higher. Perhaps lower. But consider this comparison for a moment.

According to a 2014 study by the American Bible Society, only thirty seven per cent of Americans read their Bible once a week or more (giving an indication that our values of thirty minutes a day may be generous). In comparison, according to a 2012 Nielson report, the average American spends forty hours a week watching television. This means the average American will watch over 10,000 hours of television every five years.

Where are your 10,000 hours of deliberate and intentional focus being invested?

Television? Video games? Pleasure? Leisure? A sport? A hobby? A career? Or are you choosing to intentionally and deliberately be with Jesus?

Perhaps the reason that we find it difficult to trust Jesus is because we are fail to spend time with Jesus. It has been said that one of the reasons that the average Christian is average is because too many of us give up too fast. We waste or scatter our 10,000 hours following people or things other than Christ. What about you? What will you do with your 10,000 hours?

The key to becoming a Christ-centered disciple is that Christ needs to be the center of our focus. We need to learn to hear and respond to His voice.

In order to follow Him we need to hear and accept His invitations. In order to hear and accept His invitations we must trust Him; in order to trust Him, we must invest time with Him.

The question is, how will you respond?

Reflection

1. What ideas or images stood out to you in this book?

2. What was refreshing? Why?

3. What was frustrating? Why?

4. What questions do you have?

Endnotes.

Introduction
1.(Barna 2009).
2. Matthew 11:30
3. Ephesians 4:11-15, 5:1-2

Chapter 1
1. Romans 5:8
2. Philippians 1:6, Colossians 1:10
3. 2 Timothy 2:15

Chapter 2
1. Matthew 18:17
2. Matthew 10:4, Mark 3:18, Luke 6:15

Chapter 3
1. Matthew 4:19

Chapter 4
1. Matthew 4:19
2. 1 Corinthians 1:27
3. Matthew 7:1

Chapter 6
1. Matthew 13:20-21
2. Ephesians 3:17
3. Luke 10:1
4. John 15:5
5. 1 Timothy 3:6
6. Galatians 2:20
7. John 3:30

Chapter 7
1. John 15:5
2. Luke 10:27, 1 Peter 3:15